Ken Voges and Mike Kempainen

DISCovering the Leadership Styles of Jesus

Artwork by Dan Dunn

Edited by Linda Mastaglio

ISBN 0-9703808-9-5

Printed in the United States of America
by In His Grace, Inc.

Visit us at www.inhisgraceinc.com

Dedicated to:

The Father

for giving us

His Son

and to the memory of
Susan Maddox
a co-worker at
Spring Branch Community Church
who was taken home to heaven at age 41
as the result of a tragic auto accident and
is survived by her loving husband Jimmy
and children Kara, Jake and Elijah.

About the Authors

Ken R. Voges (B.A.) is president of In His Grace, Inc., which provides believers and the church with behavioral tools and training. He was the first person to cross-reference the DISC behavioral model with biblical characters. He has since authored numerous publications integrating the styles of biblical characters with the DISC model of behavior including the book and workbook, *Understanding How Others Misunderstand You.* Ken also provides human resource consulting for Fortune 500 companies, nonprofit corporations, and churches.

Ken and his wife, Linda, are active in their local church where he teaches an adult Sunday School class and serves on the elder board. They have two children, Randy and Christy, and two granddaughters, Morgan and Peyton. Ken can be contacted by writing to: In His Grace, Inc., 3006 Quincannon, Houston, Texas 77043 or e-mail: krvoges@aol.com; www.inhisgraceinc.com

Dr. Mike Kempainen (A.B., Trinity College; Th.M., Th.D, Dallas Theological Seminary) is senior pastor at South Garland Bible Church in Garland, Texas. Mike and Ken have worked together on numerous projects involving the DISC model of behavior and biblical characters beginning with the Biblical Personal Profile.

Mike and his wife, Chrysann, have two daughters and several grandchildren. Mike can be contracted by writing to: South Garland Bible Church, 5146 South Country Club Road, Garland, Texas 75043 or by e-mail: mikekempainen@juno.com.

Contents:

Acknowledgments

Ken would like to express his gratitude to the people whose special contributions made this book possible:

Dr. Mike Kempainen for his special insights into the Scriptures.

John & Cheryl Grey, Russell Ware, Chrys Kempainen, Bill Miller and Heather Voges for reading and editing the first manuscript.

Jay Conder for providing critical insights in presenting the gospel.

Linda Voges for loving me while I labored in writing this book.

Mike would like to thank:

My wife, Chrys, who lovingly demonstrates to me the gifts of a I/S relational profile.

The Body of SBCC, who have been gracious "testers" of our model in my Sunday School classes.

Foreword

Ken Voges knows what he is writing about. First of all, Ken knows Jesus. He has been a follower of Jesus for many years and has given his focus to the study of the leadership styles of Jesus. Anything you read in this book has been hammered out in real-life faith. Ken's knowledge of Jesus is not textbook faith. It is trust in a Person who has changed his life. His coauthor, Dr. Mike Kempainen, has skillfully interpreted the biblical passages used to introduce you to the leadership styles of Jesus.

Secondly, Ken knows people. I learned the ins and outs of personality profiles from Ken. He has mentored me in my understanding of how people see the world and respond to change and pain. My ministry as a pastor has been enhanced immeasurably through what Ken has taught me. His years of experience in consulting and writing are the foundation of the personality models offered in this book. He has observed the life of Jesus with reverent awe through the lenses of this personality modeling. You can trust his insights on how Jesus interacted with others and modeled the complete human personality profile.

Thirdly, and this was new information to me, Ken knows military leaders. I was challenged and encouraged as I read the stories of the military leaders from World War II who personified each of the four basic personality profiles. Ken has described these historical characters as people we can understand. He has built sturdy bridges from these well- known leaders, to biblical leaders and finally to the leadership styles of Jesus. This is the unique characteristic of this book. You will find new interest in both these leaders and the Person of Jesus as you follow Ken's lead.

Finally, the ministry of Susan Maddox is the story defining true servant-leadership...a leadership style that always transitions to meet needs. Susan's life and servanthood beautifully bridges to the transitional styles of Jesus. The reader is challenged and encouraged to model both.

DISCovering the Leadership Styles of Jesus is a unique contribution to the writings on both leadership and Jesus. Read, learn and enjoy. I did.

C. Gene Wilkes, Senior Pastor
Legacy Drive Baptist Church
Author: *Jesus on Leadership*

Preface

In the late sixties, I first became aware of the four behavioral models through the work of Tim LaHaye. This information played a major role in saving my marriage. Since then, my passion was and has been to present behavioral information through the lives of Biblical characters and their relationship with the Lord. In 1979, I became acquainted with the DISC behavioral model through Betty Bowman. In 1984, I published the Biblical Personal Profile (BPP) which remains the cornerstone product in profiling individuals in the Bible. Since then, I have expanded the information found in the BPP into a book and workbook coauthored with Dr. Ron Braund entitled, Understanding How Others Misunderstand You.

Several years ago I had the pleasure of meeting Gene Wilkes. Through our friendship, I was honored to offer my help in integrating the DISC information in his fine work called, Jesus on Leadership. It occurred to me that expanding my insights on the leadership styles of Jesus using the DISC continuums could help readers understand the DISC behavioral model more clearly. If there ever was a true DISC servant leader model, it is found in the Carpenter from Nazareth...Jesus. This is what the book is about.

To explain DISC behavioral styles, assessments and books typically cluster words together in four groups, each describing the four styles. From past experience, I have found that if one includes a picture to enhance word descriptions of human behavior, understanding of the uniqueness of the style is more clear. In some DISC behavior books, I know authors who show themselves in four photos revealing distinctly different facial expressions. Each picture depicts a very different behavior. In the corporate community, I often use role playing videos of DISC styles in common day case studies. I have found all of these visual tools are useful in helping others understand and appreciate behavioral differences. However, these tools have their limitations because they tend to be fictional. I have found the best teaching tools to be real leaders sharing their honest problem-solving conclusions in actual case studies.

In accurately profiling someone's leadership style who is no longer living, one needs a trusted historical description of an individual's behavior in a given situation. In my opinion, the Bible remains my most trusted document for discerning unique leadership styles. If the leadership style made a positive impact in the lives of those people, the case study is invaluable to us in applying it to current situations. But, there in lies the difficulty. How, when and why do they specifically apply to your individual situation? I believe the key is in understanding and applying the eight DISC leadership models to specific case studies and linking them to real individuals and factual case studies.

To introduce each leadership style, I have used stories involving well-known 20th century political and military figures in global conflict. Through the telling of their stories, my hope is that you will to be able to more clearly understand the uniqueness of the DISC leadership styles.

Why use leaders during war time? One, because they are easily recognized and two, the stories I have used in the book associate these individuals with decisions which were made under enormous pressure and conflict. Finally, I have found that information which accurately describes how and why an individual made a difficult and stressful decision is the best validator of a person's leadership style. There are no better case studies available than ones involving leadership decisions which determined whether people groups or nations lived or died.

Most importantly, the stories have been cross-validated as a true and accurate account of what actually happened. In addition, these firsthand historical records are supplemented with visual footage (documentary film), which further assists in confirming the accuracy of a particular person's behavioral style. My initial focus is on uniquely different leaders who made decisions which influenced the saving of lives not the taking of lives. My hope is you will be able to discern clearly the value and difference in each style.

Although these individuals were different in the way they led, each had a similar respect for the sovereignty of God. My conclusion is that the Lord placed these men in positions of authority to allow their unique strengths to accomplish His work.

Once you understand the uniqueness of a particular leadership style, the stories transition to biblical characters who exhibit the same unique leadership traits as the secular leaders. Although the events are different, the problem-solving processes are the same. Finally, you will see the same styles again but this time with Jesus as the central character in each of the styles.

The more important message of the book is in being able to transition ones leadership style to best meet the need of any given situation. What is critical is in knowing what style to project to get the most positive result. In this, Jesus is the master servant- leader as shown in two additional case studies.

My hope for you, the reader, is to understand that no one leadership style is more important than another. Each has its strengths, impact qualities and limitations. The mature servant-leader understands this and discerns, with God's help, which type of behavior is most appropriate for each situation. My prayer is that you will be inspired to use these insights for shaping and expressing your personal leadership style(s).

In His Grace,

Ken Voges

The Behavioral Styles of Jesus

Each time I have taught a class or seminar on the behavioral styles of Biblical characters, someone invariably asks the question, "What was the profile of Jesus?" Gary Smalley and John Trent believe that He had the strength of all four basic personalities held in balance.[1] My good friend Dr. Robert Rohm supports this line of thinking. He says, "The life of Christ reveals the positive traits of each personality type. He was the perfect balance of all four types" [2] This is a good starting point, but this study will attempt to thoroughly investigate the DISC trait continuums to determine whether their conclusions are valid. I believe that they are.

DISC is a behavior model developed by William Marston in the early 1900's. It centers on four basic styles: "D" signifies Dominance, "I" for Influencing/Interacting, "S" for Steadiness, and "C" for Compliance/Cautious. The Dominant style desires to control the environment, whereas the Interacting/Influencer focuses on other people in building relationships. The Steadiness style values loyalty and cooperating with others whereas, the Cautious/Compliance style is compelled to do things the 'right way' or 'correct way'. This particular model has been well researched, tested for validity and is considered one of the better human resource management tools in the secular society throughout the world today.

It is important to understand that no one leadership style is necessarily better than another. Each individual style has its own set of strengths which, when left unchecked, can become unbalanced. Potential strengths can become great weaknesses. When all the styles function in concert together, balance and order have the best opportunity to occur.

It may appear to some to be bordering on blasphemy to speak of Jesus Christ as having a behavioral style or "temperament." However, one of the main doctrines of evangelical orthodoxy is the understanding of the true humanity of the Lord Jesus Christ. Not only was He undiminished deity in nature, but at the same time full humanity, though without the sin nature. Theologian John Walvoord says,"...it is necessary to view Him as having a complete human nature including body, soul and spirit."[3] If this doctrine is correct and Jesus is who He said He is, the evidence found in Scripture should show His personal profile with human behavioral traits, but always modeling balance and order.

In theory, "the DISC research evidence supports the conclusion that the most effective people are those who know themselves, know the demand of the situation, and adopt strategies to meet those needs."[4]
Although this is suggested as the ideal, no one is able to do it on a consistent basis. All of the profiles of the DISC model have imbalanced core styles that are prone to get out of control. As I associated Biblical characters with specific patterns, the behavior

of Paul, Rebekah, Abraham, Mary etc. confirmed this position. But what about Jesus' style? Does He fit into one specific pattern or does He respond according to the need of the situation with varying styles as the theoretical ideal suggests? That is the question that this study addresses.

How can one effectively research the behavior of Jesus and associate it with the DISC styles? To know how this can be done requires a basic understanding of the DISC model of behavior. It is based on a trait theory. "It classifies people according to the degree to which they can be characterized in terms of a number of traits. According to trait theory, one can describe a personality by its position on a number of scales [four continuums], each of which represents a trait."[5] The DISC Trait Continuums chart in the Understanding How Others Misunderstand You workbook[6] lists a series of 120 traits on four scales from high intensity to low intensity.

Below are examples of some of these traits:

High "D" Traits	Low "D" Traits
direct	unassuming
domineering	mild
risk-taker	modest

High "I" Traits	Low "I" Traits
persuasive	controlled
sociable	retiring
confident	aloof

High "S" Traits	Low "S" Traits
patient	mobile
loyal	spontaneous
team-person	active

High "C" Traits	Low "C" Traits
accurate	"own-person"
detailed	firm
restrained	defiant

By using this paradigm or template, we will attempt to associate Jesus' behavior among the eight High and Low styles of these four continuums. If our preliminary thesis is correct, Christ's behavior will not fit into one specific pattern, like normal individuals, but it will fill the entire chart. To be more specific, we are looking for situations where Jesus covers the entire range of DISC behavior. Our research will look at the Dominant continuum for situations where He is in charge, aggressive and confrontational in certain situations while being a loyal, submissive team player in other situations. In the Influencing continuum we will look at His ability to communicate and reach out to people yet observe when He chooses to detach Himself from some people-pressured events. In the Steadiness continuum, we will look at His patience with apostles contrasted by His spontaneous and aggressive behavior in the temple. In the Cautious continuum, we will study His restraint at His trial contrasted by His defiant and rebellious behavior towards the Jewish authorities who tried to hold Him accountable to their traditions.

If Jesus is the Son of God, the challenge will be for the DISC model to show that His behavior includes all the positive elements of all the profiles. In addition, His behavior would have to appear perfect, without imbalances, in complete control, and instantly able to take on whatever style is necessary to meet the need of each situation. Let's begin our study.

Notes:

1. Gary Smalley and John Trent, The Two Sides of Love, Focus on the Family, Pomona, CA, Copyright © 1970.

2. Robert Rohm, Positive Personality Profiles, Personality Insights, Atlanta, GA, Copyright © 1996.

3. John Walvoord, Jesus Christ Our Lord, Moody Press, Chicago, IL, Copyright © 1967, page 111.

4. The Personal Profile System, Carlson Learning Company, Minneapolis, MN, Copyright © 1977, page 1.

5. William Marston, Emotions of Normal People, Persona, Minneapolis, MN, Copyright © 1977, page xxiii.

6. Ken Voges and Ron Braund, Understanding How Others Misunderstand You workbook, In His Grace, Houston, TX, Copyright © 1990, 1994, 1999, page 27, 140.

"The life of Christ
reveals all the positive traits
of each DISC personality type.
It is my opinion that
Jesus was the perfect balance of
all the four types."

Dr. Robert Rohm

Part 1

The Diverse Leadership Styles of Jesus

Most DISC assessments profile behavior on two or three graphs. The first graph measures behavior that identifies an individual's perception of how he or she must respond in order to meet the needs of a given role. It is the most dynamic of the graphs in that it is most subject to change.

Graph I's function is to identify a person's response when considering the circumstantial demands of the focused environment; it describes the behavior an individual chooses to project in order to insure the best results. It does not necessarily measure what the person's natural style really is. Graph II's function is to describe the person's response under pressure. It generally describes the person's core style behavior. Graph III's function is to show a composite picture of Graph's I & II.

To understand specific DISC styles more clearly, we will use illustrations of familiar biblical and historical events involving actions of figures whose expression of each of the eight unique DISC styles positively influenced the course of biblical and secular history. In applying Graph I to Jesus, we will look at parallel case studies involving people caught up in highly emotional situations demanding a spontaneous but appropriate response. Comparisons will be drawn; but special focus will be on the behavior of Jesus as He handled each person's needs within the complexity of both His own and that person's circumstances. Comparisons and conclusions will be drawn between the ability of historical figures and Jesus to transition or change their behavior to meet different needs. Whereas, the other personalities tended to use one style more than any other and were not able to transition or change their behavior to meet all the needs they encountered, Jesus utilized all eight styles as needed.

While on earth, if Jesus was God yet subject to human behavior, the overwhelming evidence should show that His projected behavior in specific situations not only varied but was perfectly correct to meet the need. In addition, it should be evident from the outcome of the events that the environment Jesus created gave each individual the best chance to grow and mature.

Defining the Dominant Continuum

Power:

Having the ability to exercise authority or influence over situations or persons to insure a positive conclusion.

Control:

Having the ability to both give direction and exercise restraint over people and events.

General Douglas MacArthur

Representative Profile of
General Douglas MacArthur*

HIGH D DISC PROFILE

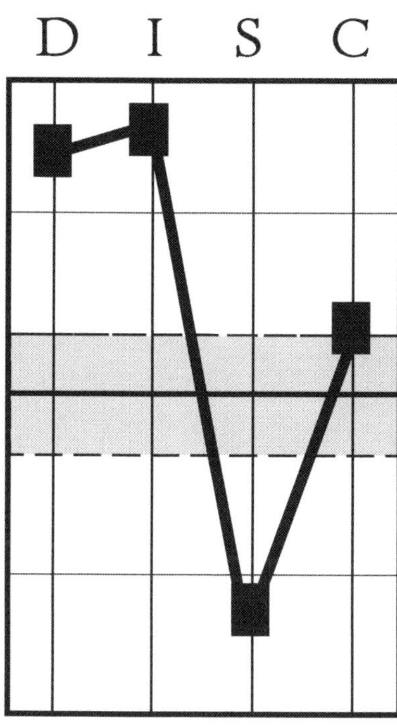

Primary Drive: Strong drive to control by charm and persuasion

Personal Giftedness: Gifted at achieving goals through dramatic presentation

Under Stress Becomes: Intimidating and can tend to manipulate others

Needs to Work on: Not having to win every argument[1]

* Based on the historical evidence, the above profile best parallels the behavior style of General MacArthur but is not intended to be absolute or final.

Notes:

1. Ken Voges & Ron Braund, Understanding How Others Misunderstand You book, ©Copyright 1990, page 96.

High D Behavior

Scriptural Case Study
Mark 5:1-20, Mark 1:21-28

For 123 generations, the people of Japan were ruled by an emperor who was considered to have been divine and possessed absolute power and control. The emperor was never seen in public nor had anyone ever heard his voice. Following his nation's defeat in WW II, Emperor Hirohito's power was severely challenged as a result of President Truman's appointment of General Douglas MacArthur as viceroy of Japan. As far as the United States was concerned, MacArthur's position gave him absolute power and authority to rule over Japan. However, to the Japanese people, his authority remained a question mark because the terms of surrender included retaining the emperor's position.

Then at the request of the emperor in early September, 1945, the two men met for the first time. The meeting was held at a neutral site, the American embassy. One picture was taken. It appeared in the local newspapers the next day. The people beheld their little sovereign standing with hat in hand beside a towering Douglas MacArthur.[1] With this public exposure, the people took ownership of the fact that a new form of power had truly arrived.

After Hirohito renounced his deity or claim to having been divine, MacArthur's natural skills of independence, decisiveness and demand for absolute authority, coupled with lordly graciousness, filled the Japanese people's need for spiritual leadership. Some Japanese went so far as to say, "We look to MacArthur as the second Jesus Christ."[2]

MacArthur yearned for power to shape, not merely implement, national policy. Being named viceroy of Japan allowed him to serve in a position that satisfied his need to exploit this desire. MacArthur preferred being in total control and exercising complete power over his environment. These traits worked well during his time in Japan.

MacArthur ruled for five years as a benevolent autocrat initially saving millions of Japanese from starvation. He also introduced numerous reforms, including the rewriting of their constitution, allowing for labor unions, providing equal rights for women and instituting land reforms. His High D expression of power met the needs of the situation. It resulted in the rebuilding of a nation totally destroyed by war. Later, in a different situation, this same style would be MacArthur's downfall.

I Kings 3:16-28
[Solomon]

"Then the king gave his ruling: 'Give the living baby to the first woman. Do not kill him; she is his mother.'"

"When all Israel heard the verdict the king had given, they held the king in awe, because they saw that he had wisdom from God to adminsiter justice."

High D traits are characteristic of individuals who impose powerful control over their environment and the people with whom they come in contact.

Word Pictures - dominant, direct, demanding, powerful, independent, authoritative, in control of the environment and intimidating.

What High D Behavior Produces in Others - a sense of fear, awe and respect knowing what the High D can do; a personal feeling of weakness when having face-to-face encounters; being terrified in their presence knowing the atmosphere and environment can be demanding and confrontational.

Solomon's Dominant Leadership Style

In exercising independent control and power over lives and events, we have the biblical example of Solomon who used his wisdom in the governing of his people.

I Kings 3 tells us that the people were still offering sacrifices at Gibeon, on the high places, because there was no "house of God" yet built. Solomon went to sacrifice there and God appeared to him in a dream and said, "Ask what you wish me to give you", (v.5). After Solomon had thanked God for His loving kindness to his father David, and to him, Solomon said, "So give thy servant an understanding heart to judge Thy people, to discern between good and evil." (v.9) Solomon acknowledged his youthfulness and inexperience and the greatness of the multitude he was to rule over. Thus he needed God's wisdom to do the job right.

In verses 11-14, we are told that Solomon's prayer pleased the Lord and He granted Solomon's wish. God also granted him that which he had not asked for, namely, earthly blessing of riches and honor.

An example of his wisdom to govern is given in verses 16-28. This is a well know account of two mothers, both harlots, who laid claim to the same child. While some dispute from linguistic consideration that they were "harlots", but rather "hostesses", since a harlot probably wouldn't be so concerned about having a child, that point is not really relevant. The point is that two mothers claimed the same child and wanted Solomon to make the decision as to who was the real mother.

They both had newborn sons, three days apart, and they lived in the same house. One of the mothers had rolled over on her infant during the night and when she discovered her son was dead, she traded her dead son for the other mother's living son as she slept. They both claimed that the other mother had done that and wanted Solomon to sort it out!

Solomon's wisdom included an understanding of motherly instincts and human behavior. His High D bottom-line style assisted in quickly determining who the real mother of the living child was. His challenge to both was rather dramatic. He said, "Bring me a sword, and we will cut the child in half, and give each mother half."

Instinctively, Solomon reasoned in his mind, that the true mother would not let any harm come to her child. He would make his decision based on the responses of the two women to the announced action plan he was about to take. The true mother immediately said to give the child to the other woman, so no harm would come to the child. However, the false mother agreed that Solomon's proposed actions were reasonable and that dividing the child in half was fair. Solomon then knew who the real mother of this child was.

The wisdom God gave to Solomon worked within the parameters of his God-given High D behavior. Someone else with a different personality might have used God's wisdom in a less dramatic and bottom-line way to decide the case.

However, in this case study, Solomon's dominant leadership style worked to produce a rather unique response from those observing the events just discussed. The crowd was awed to the point of never questioning his authority or ability to rule over people and events set before him. When this type of style is properly expressed, it tends to create an immediate, profound memory in people's minds.

Jesus Projects a Dominant Leadership Style

It is sometimes difficult to perceive Jesus projecting this type of behavior; however, when He came in contact with the demons and Pharisees, He did just that. Mark 1: 21-28 and Mark 5:2-20 give compact capsules of this type of behavior.

Jesus entered the synagogue and began to instruct the people. They were astonished at His teaching for He taught them as one having authority, but not as the scribes...the professionally trained scholars. He did not defer to the authority of others, but instead gave a more personal interpretation of the Scriptures.

In reviewing the Scriptural passages, the reader is encouraged to focus on Jesus' dominance over the demons and their response to Him. Furthermore, observe the tone and message of Christ and its impact on these demonic creatures.

Expression of Power and Absolute Control

And they went into Capernaum; and immediately on the Sabbath He entered the synagogue and began to teach.

And they were amazed at His teaching; for He was teaching them as one having authority, and not as the scribes.

And just then there was in their synagogue a man with an unclean spirit; and he cried out, saying, 'What do we have to do with You, Jesus of Nazareth? Have you come to destroy us? I know who You are—The Holy One of God!'

And Jesus rebuked him saying, 'Be quiet, and come out of him!'

And throwing him into convulsions, the unclean spirit cried out with a loud voice, and came out of him.

And they were all amazed, so that they debated among themselves, saying 'What is this? A new teaching with authority! He commands even the unclean spirits, and they obey Him.'

And immediately the news about Him went out everywhere into all the surrounding district of Galilee.

Mark 1:21-28

And when He had come out of the boat, immediately a man from the tombs with an unclean spirit met Him, and he had his dwelling among the tombs. And no one was able to bind him any more, even with a chain; because he had often been bound with shackles and chains, and the chains had been torn apart by him, and the shackles broken in pieces, and no one was strong enough to subdue him.

And seeing Jesus from a distance, he ran up and bowed down before Him; and crying out with a loud voice, he said, 'What do I have to do with You, Jesus, Son of the Most High God? I implore You by God, do not torment me!'

For He had been saying to him, 'Come out of the man, you unclean spirit!'

And He was asking him, 'What is your name?' And he said to Him, 'My name is Legion; for we are many.'

And he began to entreat Him earnestly not to send them out of the country.

Now there was a big herd of swine feeding there on the mountain side.

And they entreated Him, saying, 'Send us into the swine so that we may enter them.'

And he gave them permission. And coming out, the unclean spirits entered the swine; and the herd rushed down the steep bank into the sea, about two thousand of them were drowned in the sea.

And those who tended them ran away and reported it in the city and out in the country. And the people came to see what it was that had happened.

And they came to Jesus and observed the man who had been demon-possessed sitting down, clothed and in his right mind, the very man who had the 'legion'; and they became frightened,

And those who had seen it described to them how it had happened to the demon-possessed man, and all about the swine.

And they began to entreat Him to depart from their region.

And as He was getting into the boat, the man who had been demon-possessed was entreating Him that he might accompany Him.

And He did not let him, but He said to him, 'Go home to your people and report to them what great things the Lord has done for you, and how He had mercy on you.'

And he went off and began to proclaim in Decapolis what great things Jesus had done for him; and everyone marveled."

Mark 5:2-20

In these two passages there are eight significant elements of control mentioned regarding the situations in which Jesus found Himself.

(1) In Mark 5:6, it is mentioned that a demon-possessed man, who was mentally deranged, saw Jesus from a great distance and came running toward Him. His intent was to terrorize Jesus as he did everyone else; however, when he came closer he "fell down before Jesus." The man was controlled by legions of spirits and they caused the man to fall down and submit to Him.

(2) In verse 7, the demons pleaded for Jesus to stop tormenting them (the text shows that Jesus had been ordering the demons to depart from the man). They had no option; disobedience only resulted in further torment.

(3) In verse 10, the demons begged Jesus not to send them to another country. They were completely at His disposal.

4) In verses 12-13, the demons begged permission from Jesus to enter the swine.

5) In verse 18, the healed man requested to accompany Jesus, but was refused, and told to go home and share what Jesus had done for him.

(6) In the Mark 5 encounter, the people were "amazed" at the authoritative style of His teaching. It was on His own authority that He taught. He did not quote the teachings of former rabbis or scribes as all the other teachers did.

(7) In Mark 1:24 and Mark 5:7, the demons cried out saying , "Let us alone! What have we to do with You, Jesus of Nazareth? Did You come to destroy us? I know who You are --the Holy One of God!" The demons expressed this as a statement of fact. It is obvious the demons recognized who He was...the One who had the ultimate authority to judge them. They also said they had nothing in common with Him. Their point was that they were operating in different realms, so please leave them alone... which He did not do!

(8) In Mark 1:25, Jesus gave a simple command: "be quiet and come out" which the demons had to obey.

Jesus' Tone Throughout the Encounters

Jesus' tone was both firm and gracious. As He encountered demons, He set forth His authority in a uncompromising way. In Mark 1:25 it says "he rebuked" the demons and said "be quiet and come out." In Mark 5: 8, He says "come out...you unclean spirit." Those commands are both very firm and without wiggle room. However, the grace of the Lord even extends to these demons, where in 5:12-13 it says, "and He gave them permission" when they humbly asked to enter the swine. He didn't have to consent to their request, but He did give them permission.

The Response of the People

When the people saw the man who had been demon-possessed dressed normally and in his right mind, "they were frightened." They recognized that a supernatural event had just taken place. They then asked Jesus to leave their region! Then when the man went and shared with others what Jesus had done for him, the people "marveled." In Mark 1:27, the people in the Synagogue were "amazed", "astounded" and "profoundly impressed" at the authority present in His teaching. Their strong statement was: "What is this? A new teaching with authority, that even the unclean spirits must obey Him?" The word "new" implies new in quality as distinct from new in time. Jesus' action totally outstripped any authority they had ever seen.

Conclusion

When Jesus came in contact with demons, He consistently reflected the traits of a High D...having the power to control with absolute authority. Although they had impressive powers, the demons never challenged Him. Instead, they were terrified when in His presence. "Powerful and fearful as they are, demons are no match for the Savior, their Creator and Judge." [3] If we claim Jesus as our personal Savior, the demons have no rights or authority to influence or control us.

Notes:

1. William Manchester, American Caesar, Dell Publishing, New York, NY, Copyright© 1978, page 545.

2. Ibid, page 556.

3. C. Fred Dickason, Demon Possession and the Christian, Moody Press, Chicago, IL, Copyright© 1987, page 31.

Defining the High & Low Dominant Continuum

Independence:

Having the ability to express power and control over people and events without the influence of others.

Interdependence:

Having the ability to express power and control over people and events through the cooperation of others.

General George C. Marshall

Representative Profile of
General George C. Marshall*

LOW D DISC PROFILE

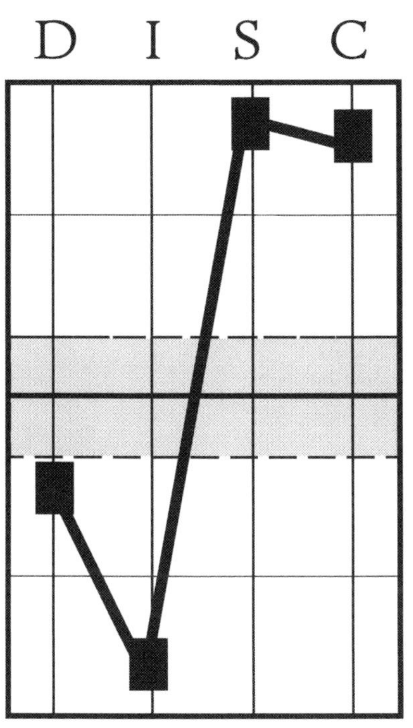

Primary Drive: Diligence in taking ownership of tasks, industrious

Personal Giftedness: Follow-through in completing tasks, tenacity

Group Giftedness: Strong administrative skills, intensely loyal

Strength Out of Control: Tends to be too direct, blunt and demanding[1]

* Based on the historical evidence, the above profile best parallels the behavior style of General Marshall but is not intended to be absolute or final.

Notes:

1. Ken Voges & Ron Braund, Understanding How Others Misunderstand You book, ©Copyright 1990, 1995, page 177.

Low D Behavior

Scriptural Case Study
Matthew 26:36-42

The date was December 4, 1943. President Roosevelt had promised Marshall Stalin a decision on who would command Operation Overlord, the invasion of Europe. It would be the most prestigious appointment of WWII. Whoever got the post could name his position after the war...including becoming President. Almost everyone's choice was George C. Marshall because he was "hands down" the most qualified...even the British and Winston Churchill agreed on that.

Roosevelt felt compelled to ask Marshall personally concerning his preferences. Marshall quietly and firmly answered, "Mr. President, I want you to feel free to act in whatever way you feel is in the best interest of the country and to your satisfaction and not in any way consider my feelings. I will cheerfully go whatever way you want me to go."[1] Roosevelt slept on it and the next afternoon summoned Marshall into his hotel suite to assist him in drafting a message which read:

From the President to Marshall Stalin,
The immediate appointment of General Eisenhower to the command of OVERLORD operation has been decided upon.
Roosevelt [2]

Roosevelt added. "I don't think I could sleep at night with you out of the country." General Marshall remained silent, asking for nothing and offering nothing in return.[3] Later he penned his own congratulations to Eisenhower on Roosevelt's original message...and as they say...the rest is history.

After the victory in Europe, Eisenhower became the most popular figure to come out of the war. He wrote his memoirs, Crusade in Europe, reaping six-figure benefits and became President in 1952.

After the war, Marshall became Secretary of State under Harry Truman and received an honorary doctorate degree from Harvard University. In his response speech, he used the event to outline a program to save Europe from economic disaster. President Truman and the European community endorsed it. Congress funded it. Later it became known as the Marshall Plan. One of its main components was sending food and basic necessities to a war-torn continent, which resulted in saving the lives of millions of people from starvation and life-threatening diseases.

On October 31, 1953, General Marshall learned that his continued selfless efforts had won him the Nobel Peace Prize. He is the only military figure to have ever received such an honor.

Luke 1:26-38
⟦Mary⟧

"The angel answered, 'The Holy Spirit will come upon you, and the power of the Most High will overshadow you, so the holy one to be born will be called the Son of God... for nothing is impossible with God.'"

" 'I am the Lord's servant,' Mary answered, 'May it be to me as you have said.'"

Whereas the High D has a desire to be in control and independent, the Low D prefers to be the selfless partner on a harmonious team. In addition, the Low D tends to project a non-confrontational spirit, the opposite of the High D.

Word Pictures - supportive, shy, soft spoken, quiet, unassuming, low key, modest, interdependent and cooperative.

What the Low D Style Produces in Others - confidence this person can be trusted to follow through and carry out a task, overwhelming presence of a selfless attitude and confidence in knowing this style represents a total team commitment.

Mary's Low Dominant Leadership Style

With regard to the ability to express power and control of people and events through cooperation with others, we have the example of Mary as she responds to the angelic announcement regarding the birth of Christ.

Beginning at the end of the dialog with the angel, Mary simply answers with the statement, "Be it done to me according to your word." It sounds so simple. A statement of compliance to the will of another. An attitude of being a team player, letting someone else make the plans. A willingness to fit in, and be helpful, fulfilling a niche that possibly no one else could fill. But, this is not the statement of a mindless, nonmotivated person just willing to go along with anything. On the contrary, Mary's mind had just been overwhelmed with some details she could scarcely believe or even understand. Yet her words, "Be it done to me according to your word."

Having appeared to Mary, the angel Gabriel told her that she had received special favor from God; that she was a person to whom God had shown His special blessing and grace.

Being a very humble, analytical person by nature, Mary was "greatly troubled" by the announcement. It literally means that she was thrown into a state of complete confusion and perplexity by the greeting. The intensity of the words show Mary's complete feelings of inadequacy at being considered someone special by God. From the point of the greeting, Mary began to think deeply about the greeting, ("kept pondering"), in order to somehow make sense of the angel's words in her mind. The imperfect tense used shows that this was not just a "fleeting thought," but rather a continuing process of mental gymnastics, trying to integrate the details of the angel's words. Her response is totally in character with her behavioral style.

Gabriel called Mary by her name and then explained that she would actually be the one to give birth to God's Son, the long-awaited Messiah, heir to the throne of David. This one to whom she would give birth would reign throughout eternity.

After Gabriel's explanation concerning her privileged status in God's plan, her only question is one of technical nature - as to the mechanics of conceiving a child while still being a virgin. Even her question was stated in a technical way, "...since I have not had intercourse with a man."

After further explanation of the mechanics of God's plan, Mary responds with to total submission in complying to God's plan with accepting obedience. She did not fully understand all that was to happen, yet her desire was to be an influence through cooperation with God's plan and the position into which God was placing her. "Be it done to me according to your word." This is within the characteristics of a person with a Low D behavior style. She allowed power and control to be expressed through cooperation.

Whereas the High D leadership style is typically expressed by action of an independent nature which often times creates an immediate, dynamic response, the Low D leadership style is more commonly not even noticed. This response only takes significance in allowing others to set in motion the team objectives. However, without the initial person's cooperation, the goals and objectives of the team could not have been accomplished. Only after the final goal is achieved is the significance of initial responding person's action realized. Even then, this type of leadership style does not draw a great deal of attention to itself, but in the final analysis, can be just as powerful.

Jesus' Low Dominant Leadership Style

The verses in Matthew 26:36-42 record the events following the last supper and preceding Christ's arrest, trial and crucifixion. Jesus takes Peter, James and John with Him to the Garden of Gethsemane. His purpose is to host a prayer vigil concerning the coming difficulties. Unfortunately, the three disciples are not supportive; instead, they fall asleep. Jesus is left alone with the Father to discuss the painful events which are about to happen.

Expression of Cooperation

Then Jesus came with them to a place called Gethsemane, and said to His disciples, 'Sit here while I go over there and pray.'

And He took with Him Peter and the two sons of Zebedee, and began to be grieved and distressed.

Then He said to them, 'My soul is deeply grieved, to the point of death; remain here and keep watch with Me.'

And He went a little beyond them, and fell on His face and prayed, saying, 'My Father, if it is possible, let this cup pass from Me; yet not as I will, but as Thou wilt.'

And He came to the disciples and found them sleeping, and said to Peter, 'So, you men could not keep watch with Me for one hour?

Keep watching and praying, that you may not

enter into temptation; the spirit is willing, but the flesh is weak.'

He went away again a second time and prayed, saying, 'My Father, if this cannot pass away unless I drink it, Thy will be done.'

And He came back and found them sleeping, for their eyes were heavy.

And He left them again, and went away and prayed a third time, saying the same things once more.

Matthew 26: 36-44

The essence of this passage is the voluntary submission of will of the God/man to the will of the Father. It states in verse 37 that Jesus began to be grieved and distressed. It implies a restless distraction, shrinking from some trouble or thought of trouble, which, nevertheless, cannot be escaped. In verse 38, the intensity escalates when it says Jesus was "deeply grieved" even to the point of death. It simply means that He was overwhelmed with the distress of the situation that He was contemplating. Another way of expressing this is, He was emotionally stressed beyond explanation.

In verse 39, Jesus prays to the Father that IF IT IS POSSIBLE, let this cup pass from Him. There are two important considerations in this verse. The first is, Jesus emotionally identifies with and describes what "this cup" is and offers His preference in wanting to pass on it. "This cup" involves taking on and suffering with all the sins of mankind that have been and will be committed, all in order that humans could be forgiven. This also involves the separation of the Father from the Son while

Jesus was on the cross. This separation, while temporary (six hours), was the only time in eternity (past or future) that the Father and Son would be separated.

The second consideration in the verse is the conditional sentence "if it is possible. . ." This is a first class condition, indicating that it indeed was possible for that cup to pass from Him. Jesus was emotionally addressing the fact that not going to the cross was an option. That, however, was not the Father's will and would have negated the saving grace of God toward man. So while Jesus was acknowledging that another path was possible for Him, he submitted to the Father's plan and will. In verse 42 Jesus introduces the condition in a different way. He uses a third class condition, indicating "more probable future," but introduces it in the negative. "If this cannot pass from me unless I drink of it", (and that is most likely true), "then not my will be done, but Yours." This delicate distinction between the conditional clauses accurately presents the real attitude of Jesus toward this subtle temptation.

His human will shrank from the suffering on a cross and His divine will shrank in having to endure the separation from the Father which would take place while He was on the cross bearing the sin of the world. (It is recorded in this passage that this dialogue with the Father took place three times and, in each case, Jesus submitted to the will of the Father to complete the plan of salvation.) The price that Jesus paid was indescribable in human terms.

Conclusion

In the High D continuum, both models of the use of power and control are valid. What allows each to work is in understanding the situation and transitioning to that style. In the examples of MacArthur and Marshall, both expressions of power, although very different, resulted in saving millions of lives. However, in the case of MacArthur, he was never able to change his way of utilizing power. In the Korean War, which involved a different set of circumstances, his inability to cooperate and submit to a higher power and authority resulted in being relieved of his position by President Harry Truman. On the other hand, Marshall's passive behavior in not mentioning a simple preference to President Roosevelt cost him the Overlord post.

Jesus continually recognized what type of expression of power and control was needed. His power and control over the demons was direct, firm, independent and absolute. His power, control and victory over sin required that He defer to the Father's will and voluntarily give up His life so that we might be forgiven by the Father. Without this selfless action, we would remain lost with no hope of a relationship with God the Father.

Notes:

1. Ed Cray, General of the Army, George C. Marshall, Soldier and Statesman, Touchstone Book, New York, NY, Copyright© 1990, page 446.

2. David Eisenhower, Eisenhower at War 1943-1945, Vintage Books, New York, NY, Copyright © 1987, page 45.

3. Ibid, page 45.

Defining the Influencing Continuum

People

Having the ability to respond to people's needs, issues and events.

Relationships

Having the ability to emotionally connect with people for the purpose of mutual edification.

Sir Winston Churchill

Representative Profile of
Sir Winston Churchill *

HIGH I DISC PROFILE

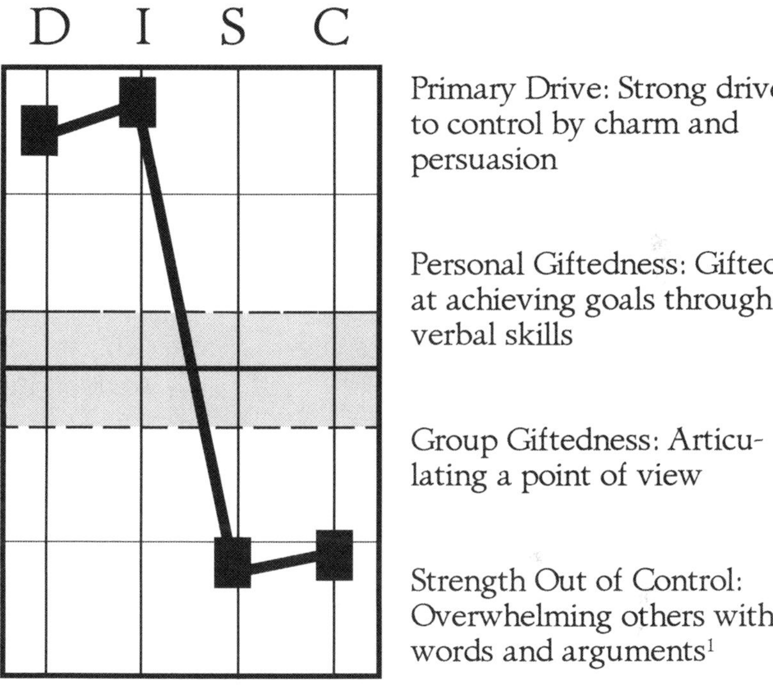

Primary Drive: Strong drive to control by charm and persuasion

Personal Giftedness: Gifted at achieving goals through verbal skills

Group Giftedness: Articulating a point of view

Strength Out of Control: Overwhelming others with words and arguments[1]

* Based on the historical evidence, the above profile best parallels the behavior style of Churchill but is not intended to be absolute or final.

Notes:

1. Ken Voges & Ron Braund, Understanding How Others Misunderstand You book, ©Copyright 1990, page 96.

High I Behavior

Scriptural Case Study
Matthew 14:13-21,
Mark 6:30-44,
John 6:1-14

While the British War Cabinet was meeting on May 17,1940, word came that the French had surrendered. England was now alone. Some British leaders, including Lord Halifax and Neil Chamberlain, suggested responding to Hitler's appeal for a negotiated settlement to end the hostilities between England and Germany.

Winston Churchill, England's new Prime Minister, would have none of that. One of his greatest gifts was the ability to use his exceptional mastery of words, and love of language, to convey detailed arguments and essential truths; to inform, to convince, and to inspire.[1]

The next day, Churchill made one of the most memorable speeches ever given in the House of Commons--an address which was later broadcast to the nation. The follow are excerpts from that speech:

"Upon this battle depends the survival of Christian civilization. Upon it depends our own British life and the long continuity of our institutions and our Empire. The whole fury and might of the enemy must very soon be turned on us. Hitler knows that he will have to break us in this island or lose the war. If we can stand up to him, all Europe may be free, and the life of the world may move forward into broad, sunlit uplands; but if we fail, then the whole world, including the United States, and all that we have known and cared for, will sink into the abyss of a new dark age made more sinister, and perhaps more protracted, by the lights of a perverted science.

"Let us therefore brace ourselves to our duty and so bear ourselves that if the British Empire and its Commonwealth lasts for a thousand years men will say, 'This was their finest hour.'"[2] It was!

The whole House cheered him. Later when he was asked whether he wanted to respond to Hitler's offer to negotiate with Britain for an end to the war, his answer was: 'I do not propose to say anything in reply to Herr Hitler's speech, not being on speaking terms with him.'[3]

In addition to his verbal encouragement, Churchill would daily walk among the people touching, encouraging and consoling them. Because of Churchill's continued inspiration, the British people never wavered in their resolve. He did what he could for them, when he could, by providing food and shelter, but often retreating to his car in tears.

Acts 3 & 4
⟦Peter⟧

When Peter healed the lame man, he went around the temple walking and jumping and praising God... And the people gathered around and were filled with wonder and amazement at what had happened to him.

"When Peter saw this, he said to them: 'Men of Israel why does this surprise you? ...It is Jesus' name and the faith that comes through Him that has given this completed healing to him, as you can all see...repent then, and turn to God'...and many who heard the message believed and the number of men grew to about five thousand."

High I tendencies are characterized by an individual who desires a relationship with people. High I's typically are excellent communicators, using word pictures to express their ideas and feelings.

Word Pictures - inspiring, influencing others with words of assurance and hope, interactive by socializing with the masses, gifted at sensing the needs of others and setting in motion positive energy and action to meet needs.

What the High I Profile Produces in Others - when in their presence, a feeling of being shepherded by a person who cares, reassurance, accepting environments, a sense of encourage ment and hope in times of despair.

Peter's Influencing Leadership Style

The gift of the High I is the ability to focus on "people" issues in social settings to meet needs. The incident in Acts 3 represents a clear example of that ability, as displayed in Peter's actions.

The setting was not unusual. Peter and John were on their way to pray in the Temple when they came across a man, lame from birth, begging alms in front of the Temple gate. He was asking for, and hoping for, some monetary gift from the two men. What happened next shows the social, interpersonal skills of Peter's High I personality.

V. 4-6 - Catching the man's attention, Peter said, "Look at us". This is a strong word which meant "Look here, now!" Having the man's undivided attention, Peter said that they didn't have money, but had something even better from Jesus Christ.

Then he said (v. 6), "In the name of Jesus Christ the Nazarene - walk!" This word is another imperative, meaning to walk around, to start moving.

V. 7 - Peter then showed the "hands on" tendency of the high I by "seizing him by the right hand, he raised him up." This was no "let me help you up" kind of action. The word "seize" here means "to seize and take into custody." It is used of the authorities arresting someone and even has the idea of "pouncing upon" someone in one passage. The text says that when Peter had "yanked" him to his feet, his feet and ankles were strengthened. The man then began to run and leap and praise God, getting the attention of all who knew him to be lame from birth.

V. 11- The reaction of the people was one of amazement, which became a crucial test for Peter. The attention was now upon Peter and John as to the origin of the miracle.

V. 13 - With his outstanding verbal skills, Peter pointed to God and to Jesus Christ as the means and cause of the miracle, while not taking the credit. He then preached a sermon on how the crowd had disowned Jesus, delivering Him up to be crucified. The Holy and Righteous One, they had rejected in favor of a criminal thus creating a need to repent. He skillfully communicates that only through faith in Jesus name can one be delivered from sin. (v. 16)

V. 17 - With Peter's outstanding people-focused leadership style, he softened his verbal attack by saying "this you did in ignorance, as did your leaders." He tells them how the prophets and Moses had predicted the coming of Jesus Christ and that they needed to repent and believe in His Name.

Peter, focusing on the real need of the lame man, used his physical need to bring him to Christ, his real need. Then Peter deflected the response of the crowd toward their need of the Savior. They were guilty of the death of Jesus Christ, but they could be forgiven by repentance and faith in Christ. The result was astounding. Five thousand men came to Christ in faith, (not to mention women and children), because of Peter's sermon.

In the case study of Peter, the Influencing leadership style has the ability reach out to people in a unique way so that the very core of ones emotional security needs are met. This style also has the ability to follow-up with a sensitive, inspirational message that can cause individuals to want to take whatever action the speaker is suggesting.

Jesus' High Influencing Leadership Style

Jesus verbally projected His High I skills in His use of parables...or stories related to common experiences...but with moral or spiritual meaning. Jesus used this method along with other kinds of figures of speech.

How Jesus Expressed High I Traits in Relating to People

He also took the time to reach out to people whenever needs were present. Matt. 14:10-21 records one of these examples. After hearing about the murder of John the Baptist, Jesus desired to be alone. Jesus, however, was encountered by a large multitude of people, who had come to interact with Him.

And when He came out, He saw a great multitude, and felt compassion for them, and healed their sick.

And when it was evening, the disciples came to Him, saying, 'The place is desolate, and the time is already past; so send the multitudes away, that they may go into the villages and buy food for themselves.

But Jesus said to them, 'They do not need to go away; you give them something to eat!'

And they said to Him, "We have here only five loaves and two fish.'

And He said, 'Bring them here to Me.'

And ordering the multitudes to recline on the grass, He took the five loaves and the two fish, and looking up toward heaven, He blessed the food, and breaking the loaves He gave them to the disciples, and the disciples gave the food to the multitudes, and they all ate, and were satisfied. And they picked up what was left over of the broken pieces, twelve full baskets.

And there were about five thousand men who ate, aside from women and children."

Matthew 14:14-21

Both Matthew and Mark record that He was moved with "compassion" when He saw the multitude of people. Both use the same word, which means "to have pity", "to be moved with compassion", "to feel sympathy" for someone. The word comes from a root that literally means "to have one's inner parts churning", and is translated "bowels" from the old idea that emotions came out of the organs. There were two things that concerned Jesus about this multitude.

(a) Matthew says that He had compassion and healed their sicknesses.

(b) Mark mentions that His compassion was centered around the fact that they were as "sheep without a shepherd" and that Jesus taught them many things. This aspect of His concern is reflected in Mt. 9:36, (which on another occasion, reflects His concern for the people), "And seeing the multitudes, He felt compassion for them, because they were distressed and downcast like sheep without a shepherd."

While Jesus was teaching the multitude, it began to get late into the afternoon, and they would need something to eat. The disciples wanted to send the crowd away, but Jesus wanted to meet the need. Mark's report says that it was "already quite late", while Matthew says "when it was evening". The Jewish day understood two different "evenings", the first beginning at 3:00 p.m., while the second was at sundown. This event occurred about 3:00 p.m. and the people were in need of food. It became for Jesus a way to "kill two birds with one stone": a provision for the people, and a lesson for the disciples. The Lord told His disciples to feed the people, so they could see it was humanly impossible, but He intended to miraculously feed the people all along.

But this He said to test him [Philip], for He Himself knew what He would do.

John 6:6

This resulted in a dual-purpose encounter, meeting the physical needs of the multitude and the spiritual needs of the disciples.

In Matthew 14 it states that He instructed the people to recline on the grass. He used a word which generally designates verbal instructions from a superior. The people understood the status of their teacher and they obeyed. They were seated in ordered rows which was customary of students with a rabbi. He fed 5,000 men, women and children with five loaves of bread and two fish. It was a marvelous time of fellowship, a wonderful picnic, and a great conclusion to a special day of enlightenment filled with positive surprises and fun!

Jesus' Tone Throughout These Encounters

Jesus' tone and style with the masses tended to be both relaxed and friendly. He often taught by sitting down while enjoying a meal. His method of teaching tended to be stories and illustrations taken from daily events. Jesus was a master at using words to create pictures. He also tended to focus on each facet of a person's life. His passion was to develop a relationship with each individual by meeting whatever need was presented.

The Response of the People

According to John 6:14, the people responded to the feeding by saying, "Surely this truth is of the prophet who is to come into the world." This miracle led them to identify Him with the Messianic association. However, they did not understand fully what that Messianic designation called for according to the Old Testament Prophets. Instead, their spontaneous desire was to force Him into being a political force who would lead them in overthrowing the Roman government.

Conclusion

When Jesus related to the needs of people, He

consistently reflected the traits of a High I...he communicated through parables (word pictures), and consistently projected a shepherd's heart in offering hope to the multitudes of people who were living in a time of misery and despair. However, the people's reactions in John 6:15 required Him to change His strategy to that of a Low I.

Notes:

1. Martin Gilbert, Churchill A Life , Henry Holbert and Company Touchstone Book, New York, NY, Copyright© 1991, page xx.

2. John Strawson, Churchill and Hilter, In Victory and Defeat, Fromm International, New York, NY, Copyright© 1997, page 274.

3. Ibid, page 279.

Defining the High & Low Influencing Continuum

Interpersonal

Ability to focus on *people* issues in social settings to meet needs.

Introspective

Having the ability to maintain focus on what is *best* for the people rather than respond to what the people say they want.

President Harry S Truman

Representative Profile of
President Harry S Truman*

LOW I DISC PROFILE

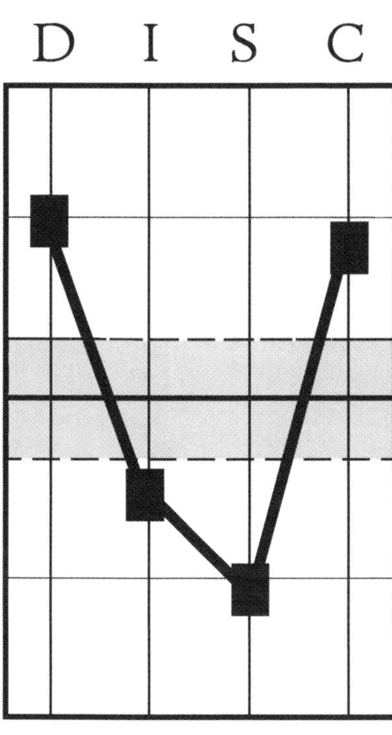

Primary Drive: Being the front runner developing new concepts

Personal Giftedness: Being the instrument to bring about change

Group Giftedness: Going against the majority in making bold decisions

Needs to Work on: Communicating warmth while softening a critical spirit[1]

* Based on the historical evidence, the above profile best parallels the behavior style of President Truman but is not intended to be absolute or final.

Notes:

1. Ken Voges & Ron Braund, Understanding How Others Misunderstand You book, ©Copyright 1990, 1995 page 98.

Low I Behavior

Scriptural Case Study
Matthew 14:22-23
Mark 6:45-46
John 6:15

On Saturday November 29, 1947, the United Nations, including representatives of the United States, voted for the partitioning of Palestine. Britain also announced that responsibility for Palestine would be turned over to the United Nations on May 14, 1948.[1] The Arabs said partition meant war. The dilemma for the President and the US was whether or not to officially recognize the new Jewish state and risk war in the middle east.

The State Department, now headed by George Marshall, the architect of the Marshall Plan, was solidly against recognition. Marshall's fear was not only war but the boycotting of oil shipments to both the US and Europe by the Arab region. Furthermore it was estimated that 100,000 US troops would be needed to keep the peace.

Truman had a different view. He was a man steeped in both the Old and New Testaments. He reasoned that he might help to end 2,500 years of wandering by the Lord's chosen people and do justice in the wake of the Holocaust.[2] A meeting between the President and the State Department was held on May 12 to discuss the issue. The President needed Marshall's support. In the meeting, Marshall strongly argued against recognition and Clark Clifford, one of the President's legal experts, argued strongly for it. The tone of the meeting turned from seething anger to ice cold confrontation. General Marshall directly rebuked Truman by suggesting that if the President were to follow Clifford's advice, and if in the elections in November (1948), he, Marshall, were to vote, he would vote against the President.[3] It was the sharpest rebuke Truman ever received from a man he deeply respected. To lose Marshall's support would surely doom any hope of being reelected President. The room grew deathly silent only to be relieved by Marshall's exit.

Truman felt in his heart that recognizing Israel was the right decision. Should he do that, Truman feared Marshall would resign, casting a death sentence on his reelection. However, he decided to go ahead. On the morning when recognition was to be announced, General Marshall called Truman to say that while he could not support the position the President wished to take, he would not oppose it publicly.[3] That was all Truman needed. At ten o'clock Washington time on May 15, 1948, the Nation of Israel declared its independence. Eleven minutes later, the White House announced that the President had granted full and unconditional recognition.[4] The United States was the first nation to do so. Israel was a nation again after 2,000 years!

Marshall was under enormous pressure to speak out publicly against the President's actions and/or resign. His answer to these inputs was, "No, gentlemen, you don't take a post of this sort and then resign when the man who has the constitutional responsibility to make decisions makes one you don't like."[5] Marshall kept his word and saw to it that no one resigned.

Truman, on the other hand, felt great satisfaction in what he was able to do for the Jewish people and was deeply moved by their continued affirmation. When the Chief Rabbi of Israel, Isaac Halevi Herzog, visited the White House, he told Truman, "God put you in your mother's womb so you would be the instrument to bring the rebirth of Israel after two thousand years."[6]

One of Truman's aides thought it was a little much, but when he looked at the President, tears were running down his checks. This one decision was among the most meaningful to him personally. He also won re-election in 1948.

Whereas the High I prefers to work with people, the Low I is very comfortable working alone. What makes the Low I traits so unique is the abililty to focus on the facts of issues, whereas the High I decisions are too often influenced by social pressure and politically-correct responses. Truman personified Low I traits in this incident. After Truman made his decision, Marshall also projected the traits of the Low I by supporting the President.

I Samuel 15:1-34
[Samuel & Saul]

"When Samuel reached him, Saul said, 'The Lord bless you! I have carried out the Lord's instructions.'

"But Samuel said, ' What then is this bleating of sheep in my ear? What is this lowing of cattle that I hear?'

"Until the day Samuel died, he did not go to see Saul again, though Samuel mourned for him. And the Lord was grieved that he had made Saul king over Israel."

The Low I traits are characteristic of individuals who maintain their composure and stay firm in their commitment to agreed upon goals and objectives.

Word Pictures - conscientious, contemplative, careful, when alone, has a tendency to spend the time in reassessing objectives, goals and direction; has the ability to stand firm on principles rather than being pressured by the masses to compromise; doing what's right, not what's politically correct.

What the Low I Style Produces in Others - confidence in being able to count on them to be objective and in control of their emotions when everyone else isn't; a model of consistency; inspiring confidence that their decisions are well thought out and based on facts and solid principles.

Samuel's Low Influencing Leadership Style

The gift of the Low Influencing leadership style is having the ability to maintain focus on what is 'best' for the people rather than respond to what the people say they desire or want. I Samuel 15 gives a contrast between King Saul, the High I, who was not able to withstand being pressured by the people versus Samuel, the Low I, who was able to hold Saul and the people accountable for not carrying out the instructions of the Lord.

Vs. 1-4 The Children of Israel had been attacked and harassed by the Amalekites from the time they had wandered in the wilderness and the harassment had continued in the land. Therefore, God gave Saul a simple and clear mission--to completely annihilate the Amalekites, every human, every animal and all their possessions. Further, Saul was given an army of 210,000 men to accomplish the task.

Vs. 5-9 Saul took on the task, but did not follow the instructions. He let Agag, the king of the Amalekites live and saved the best of the animals from the slaughter.

Vs. 10-12 God's word came to Samuel the prophet, saying that Saul had disobeyed God, that God regretted making Saul the King of Israel because Saul had disobeyed Him. Samuel prayed and poured out his distress over this matter all night.

V. 13 - In the morning, Samuel went to Saul, and Saul pretended nothing was wrong by giving him a cheery greeting. Then he said, "I have carried out the command of the Lord."

V. 14 – Samuel immediately pointed out Saul's lie. He said, "Why then, do I hear the bleating of sheep and the lowing of oxen?" In other words, "you are not telling the truth!"

v. 15 – Saul immediately went into the common High I trait of shifting the blame when caught in a transgression. "They...the people...did this, not me, but it was for a good cause. They saved the good stuff so that they could sacrifice it to God. "But the rest, we have utterly destroyed." The indication from the text is that "the rest" refers to animals that were diseased and useless.

v. 16-19 - Samuel did not even give credence to Saul's excuse but went straight to the word from God.

> "Here is what God has told me. . ."
> -God made you to be king
> -God sent you on a mission
> -You disobeyed.

V. 20-21 Saul again excuses himself. I obeyed, but the people did not.

Vs. 22-23 Samuel again disregards Saul's excuses and says: God wants obedience, not sacrifice. Because you rejected the Word of God, God has rejected you from being king.

Vs. 24-28 Saul confesses and repents, but Samuel sticks to God's word to him and says "God has torn the kingdom from you."

It took an incredible amount of clear thinking and focus for Samuel to stay on track with Saul. Saul had many excuses, explanations, and claims to have obeyed God's instructions. Saul finally even confessed his sin, repented and begged for Samuel's backing. But Samuel stood firm on the word that came to him from God.

Jesus' Low Influencing Leadership Style

Following the miracle of the feeding of the 5,000, the people, with the support of the disciples, moved toward making Jesus their King.

When therefore the people saw the sign which He had performed, they said, 'This is of a truth the Prophet who is to come into the world.'

Jesus therefore perceiving that they were intending to come and take Him by force, to make Him king, withdrew again to the mountain by Himself alone.

John 6:14-15

According to John's account, the response of the multitude to the miraculous meal was twofold.

(a) They saw Jesus as a candidate for their Messianic hopes. They identified Him with an idea they had of the Messiah, who they referred to as "The Prophet" that is to come into the world. (see Deut 18:15-19) While we know that all Israel was longing for their Messiah at this time, their expectations over the centuries had deteriorated into a political savior who would bring them victory over the Roman rule which held them captive.

(b) Jesus "perceived" what they intended. The word simply means "he knew" what they were about to do. In His omniscience, Jesus recognized that their intention was to try to set Him up as political king. It says they intended to "seize" Him. This is a very violent word which has the connotations of brute force. They were going to force the Messiah to be their political king!

Expressions of Introspection

Both Matthew and Mark say that Jesus responded immediately. He quickly sent the disciples away in a boat. The word means to compel or to force, showing the urgency of the situation. Jesus didn't want his disciples involved, so he provided a way for them to leave, before the intentions of the crowd could be seen.

Before the crowd could get organized, or come up with some leaders in this cause, He sent them away. Sending them away was accomplished in a positive manner, as Mark records "after bidding them farewell, He departed to the mountain." Again, Jesus' action was not negative, but it was immediate. Jesus allowed for a cooling down of this emotional high. For the record, that spontaneous affirmation of His activities is a High I's dream. Jesus had to set aside this positive response of the people, no matter how genuine, and dismiss them in order to re-focus on his real mission of going to the cross.

He then withdrew to the mountain to pray. He wanted to be without human companionship, because

He wanted to be alone with His Father. The word used expresses purpose. He wasn't just trying to get away from the crowd and the disciples, His purpose in going to the mountain was to pray to the Father. This was not a result of the situation, but His purpose in the situation.

Conclusion

In the High I continuum, both styles involve people issues. One remains sensitive to what other people feel; the other requires more objectivity, always considering the long-term implications. In the examples of Churchill and Truman, both expressions of people issues were very different and both effectively met the need. However, one of Churchill's major flaws was his inability to separate from the emotion attached to critical decisions. He often made errors by seeking the advice of inspired amateurs, much to the dismay of his military advisors His staff would constantly be called upon for damage control. Truman, on the other hand, was legendary for his lack of tact and bluntness with the press.

When Jesus had to respond to issues involving His mission on earth, He consistently was dependent on the Father rather than giving in to the expectations of the people. He continually spent time alone with the Father to insure that they were together on a plan. Behaviorally, this best reflects the traits of a Low I.

Notes:

1. David McCullough, Truman, Simon & Schuster, New York, NY ©Copyright 1992, page 602.

2. Ed Cary, General of the Army, George C. Marshall, Soldier and Stateman, Simon & Schuster, New York, NY ©Copyright 1990, page 659.

3 . David McCullough, Truman, Simon & Schuster, New York, NY ©Copyright 1992, page 616.

4. Ed Cary, General of the Army, George C. Marshall, Soldier and Stateman, Simon & Schuster, New York, NY ©Copyright 1990, page 661.

5. Ibid page 661.

6. David McCullough, Truman, Simon & Schuster, New York, NY ©Copyright 1992, page 620.

7. John Keegan, Who was Who in World War II, Thomas Crowell Publishers, New York, NY, ©Copyright 1978, page 60.

Defining the Steadiness Continuum

Predictability

Having the ability to foresee and implement a course of action which produces an expected result.

Patience

Having the ability to remain calm and steady under pressure with a willingness to assume blame for others.

General Dwight D. Eisenhower

Representative Profile of
General Dwight D. Eisenhower *

HIGH S DISC PROFILE

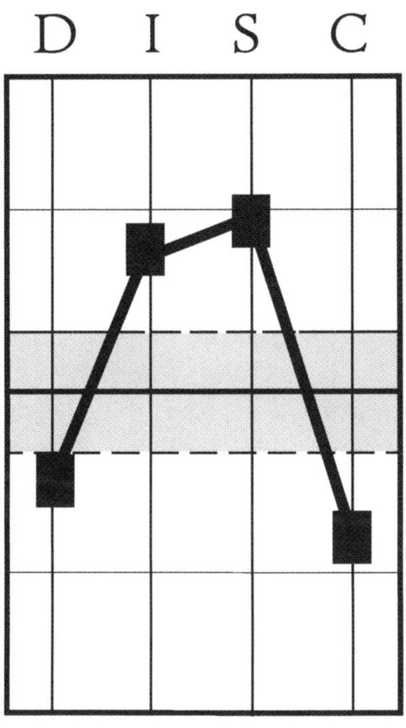

Primary Drive: Maintaining peace and harmony

Personal Giftedness: Loyalty to friends, friendliness, peacemaker

Group Giftedness: Bringing together opposing groups of people for a common cause

Under Stress Becomes: Accommodating, internalizes conflict[1]

* Based on the historcial evidence, the above profile best parallels the behavior style of General Eisenhower but is not intended to be absolute or final.

Notes:

1. Ken Voges & Ron Braund, Understanding How Others Misunderstand You book, ©Copyright 1990, 1995 page 179.

High S Behavior

Scriptural Case Study
Matthew 26:31-35
Luke 22:37
Matthew 26:69-75
Luke 22:61-62

General George S. Patton Jr. was a genius at waging war. He was also gifted at opening his mouth and saying the wrong thing at the wrong time. Patton had a knack of turning a local indiscretion into a worldwide crisis in record time. His Welcome Club speech on April 25, 1944 at Knutsford, England was a classic example.

His remarks before a small group of English ladies was dramatized fairly accurately in the motion picture "Patton." The statement that got him into trouble was "since it is the evident destiny for the British and Americans, and of the Russians to rule the world, the better we know each other, the better job we will do."[1] He was told no reporters would be present, but he soon learned that there were. Unfortunately, some of the British accounts failed to mention the Russians. Of course, the wire services picked up the story quoting Patton saying that Britain and the United States were destined to rule the postwar world. Hence a major world crisis ensued.

Patton's perceived faux pas could not have come at a worse time for Marshall who had submitted a list of generals to Congress for promotion. Of course, Patton's name was on it along with Bedell Smith, Ike's Chief of Staff. The media fueled the controversy and Washington, including Congress, became outraged and wanted Patton's scalp. Between April 27 and May 3, six rather frantic communications between Marshall and Eisenhower's headquarters were exchanged. Unfortunately, because of Ike's absence, Bedell Smith handled the initial inquiry from Marshall and overreacted, thus making the situation worse. Cooler heads were needed and Eisenhower and Marshall eventually prevailed.

When Eisenhower first became aware of the situation, he was intent on sending Patton home, but his patience and deliberate investigation shed new light on the matter. The evidence showed Patton had indeed declined to speak, but under the insistence of his hosts agreed to say a word or two in support of the gathering. The second point was that he had been assured that the meeting was a private one, with no reporters present and that no information concerning its details would be given to anyone.[2]

On May 1, Patton had his contrite meeting with Ike. Patton offered to resign but Eisenhower dismissed the idea suggesting that he might yet need his services to command an army. However, pressure from Washington, particularly Marshall, was so great that he, Eisenhower, might be obliged to send him home. But a decision had not yet been made. Patton was devastated as he left Eisenhower's office.

On May 2, with great forbearance and wisdom, Marshall reaffirmed that Patton's future lay in Eisenhower's hands alone. His cable read:

THE DECISION IS EXCLUSIVELY YOURS, MY VIEW, THAT YOU SHOULD NOT WEAKEN YOUR HAND FOR OVERLORD, IF YOU THINK THAT PATTON'S REMOVAL DOES WEAKEN YOUR PROSPECT, YOU SHOULD CONTINUE HIM IN COMMAND...CONSIDER ONLY OVERLORD AND YOUR OWN HEAVY BURDEN OF RESPONSIBILITY FOR ITS SUCCESS. EVERYTHING ELSE IS OF MINOR IMPORTANCE.[3]

On May 4, Eisenhower made his decision and sent Patton a cable: I AM ONCE MORE TAKING THE RESPONSIBILITY OF RETAINING YOU IN COMMAND IN SPITE OF DAMAGING REPERCUSSIONS RESULTING FROM A PERSONAL INDISCRETION. I DO THIS SOLELY BECAUSE OF MY FAITH IN YOU AS A BATTLE LEADER AND FROM NO OTHER MOTIVES.[4]

Patton tearfully breathed a huge sigh of heartfelt relief. He quickly cabled his wife with the following message: "EVERYTHING IS AGAIN OK BECAUSE DIVINE DESTINY CAME THROUGH IN A BIG WAY. "[5] Patton felt he was destined for some great thing but did not know what it was. His two patient, supportive friends saved him again but he rightfully gave credit to the Lord. His work was not done.

I Samuel 25: 2-42
[Abigail, Nabal & David]

"One of the servants told Nabal's wife, Abigail, 'David sent messengers from the desert to give our master greetings, but he hurled insults at them. Yet these men were very good to us. They did not mistreat us, and the whole time we were out in the field near them nothing was missing.' "

"David's men turned around and went back. When they arrived, they reported every [insulting] word. David said to his men, 'Put on your swords!' And David put on his. About 400 men went up with David."

[David intended to kill Nabal, his family and servants and take all their possessions.]

High S tendencies of an individual are expressed by incredible patience and constancy. Even in adversity, they have the tendency to be extremely loyal to members of their team.

> Word Pictures - supportive, stable, steady, patient, loyal, gifted peacemaker, good at follow-through yet willing to make allowances for mistakes.

> What the High S Style Produces in Others - harmony, assurance that here is someone you can count on to be your friend when things are bad, a sense of security in knowing you can make a mistake but will not be rejected.

Abigail's Steadiness Leadership Style

While there are a number of characteristics which define the Steadiness leadership style, two important factors are loyalty and discernment (the ability to see the big picture). These two characteristics stand out in Abigail, the wife of Nabal. The story of David's encounter with Nabal in I Samuel 25 uncovers these characteristics in Abigail, (and saved her husband's life, at least for a while.)

The background is that David and his men had shown wonderful hospitality and kindness for some of Nabal's shepherds, but when it came time to return the favor, Nabal thumbed his nose at David's request. This sent David on a crusade to eliminate Nabal and his men from the privilege of life!

Thus enters Abigail on the scene to intercept David and save the worthless life of her husband, Nabal. A person without Abigail's loyalty would have sat back and watched Nabal get what was coming to him. Verses 18-28 show this tremendous loyalty on Abigail's part. When she heard of how Nabal had slighted David, and that David was on his way to exact revenge, she put together a gourmet meal (v. 18) and intercepted David before he could get to Nabal. After she presented all the food to David, she took the blame upon herself (v. 23-24) for the situation, and asked for a chance to explain. Abigail then pointed out the type of person her husband was. She said he was a "worthless man" and just like his name, (which means "fool".)

Abigail then covered for Nabal's mistake by saying, "I didn't see the young men that you sent," so please take this gift of food and do not shed blood (which you may regret). In verses 36-38 we are given a glimpse of the depth of loyalty Abigail showed toward Nabal. When she got to the house after dealing with David, Nabal was putting on a party and was very drunk. Therefore Abigail waited until morning, when he was sober, to relate to him how close he had come to death at David's hand. The next morning, when she told him, "his heart died within him, and he became a stone." Some think this means that he suffered a stroke and was paralyzed. Nabal died ten days later as a judgment from God.

David himself points out Abigail's discernment, her ability to see the big picture. (vs. 32-34) David said, ". . .blessed be your discernment, and blessed be you, who have kept me this day from bloodshed. . ." David then said that if Abigail had not stepped in when she did, Nabal and all his men would not have seen the light of day. Abigail also pointed out to David that God would one day make him king of Israel and his response should keep that in sight. (v. 28-30)

The wisdom of Abigail's loyalty and discernment can be seen in the outcome of her dealings with David. In verse 32 he says, "you kept me from bloodshed." In verse 35, David says "Go up to your house in peace. See, I have listened to you and have granted your request." In verse 39 it says that when David learned that Nabal was dead, he requested for Abigail to come and be one of his wives. This amazing outcome was the result of the natural instincts of Abigail to be loyal and to see the "big picture."

In the case study of Abigail, the Steadiness leadership style showed the ability to remain patient and loyal despite the insensitivity of partners, superiors, co-workers or subordinates. This behavioral style may even assume blame for the actions of others in order to prevent the escalation of negative responses and destructive events.

Jesus' High Steadiness Leadership Style

Following the last supper and the singing of a hymn, Jesus said, "You will all fall away because of Me this night, for it is written, I will strike down the shepherd, and the sheep of the flock shall be scattered, but after I have been raised, I will go before you into Galilee."

Expression of Support Through Patience:

In the Matthew 26:31-32 passage, Jesus was trying to prepare His disciples for the coming events by giving a simple warning with a hopeful message. His message was:

(1) He would be struck down and all of his disciples would flee. The passive voice of the verb shows that they would flee but not of their own choosing.

(2) Their fleeing of the scene would fulfill the prophecy of Zechariah 13:7.

(3) Then He would be raised from the dead, and meet them in Galilee. The grammar signifies a necessary order of events, which the Lord is trying to convey to His disciples.

No one was asked to comment; simply to listen. Unfortunately, Peter's mind reacted and his mouth became engaged and he spoke.

In verse 33, "Peter answered and said to Him 'Even though all may fall away because of You, I will never fall away.'"

Peter's comment uses an emphatic "I" to contrast himself against the other disciples. He also uses a kind of future tense that expresses a determination of the will. He was certainly serious about his intentions, just not listening to what the Lord was saying!

In verse 34, Jesus said to him, "Truly I say to you that this very night before a cock crows, you shall deny Me three times..."

Jesus responds by setting a time...the cock crowing marked the Roman third watch (3-6 a.m.). Jesus uses a compound word that signifies not only denial, but a total, complete denial.

In verse 35, Peter says, "Even if I have to die with you..." In Peter's mind, his dying with Jesus was a real possibility.

In Luke 22:31-32, again Jesus responds to Peter with undeserved patience, "Simon, Simon, Satan has demanded permission to sift you like wheat; but I have prayed for you that your faith may not fail; and you, when once you have turned again, strengthen your brothers."

In these two verses, we get insight into the spiritual struggle that was taking place with the disciples, and the intense oversight the Son of God was giving to His men. Jesus states that Satan had 'demanded permission" to sift the disciples, like wheat. The word used only here in the New Testament has the understanding of "obtaining by asking". It is in the middle voice which means that Satan had a personal interest in the matter. Satan wanted to "test" the disciples to the limit of God's allowance. Peter, as the leader of the group of men was probably the focus of the attack by the enemy; therefore, Jesus encouraged Peter with the words "but I have prayed for you." Satan wanted to sift all of the disciples, and Jesus prayed specifically for Peter. The word Jesus used for prayer has the idea in its root of binding. He was binding Himself to Peter for the strength of Peter's faith and that it would not fail. Peter's faith didn't fail, but his hope did, and the prayer of Jesus would bring back the vitality of Peter's faith. He was to use his strengthened faith to encourage his disciples.

My personal experience is that sifting by Satan goes on all the time. The strong message here is that we need to pray constantly for our leaders so that they will have the strength and wisdom to withstand the sifting and to maintain focus on the Lord.

Jesus re-emphasized the need for the prophecies concerning Him to be fulfilled. Here He refers to Isaiah 53:12. This must happen, where He would be classified with sinners and " bear the sins of many."

Following Jesus' arrest and during His trial, Matthew records that Peter initially offered a simple denial, then moved away from the lighted area of the gate, so he would not be recognized. In verse 72 of Matthew 26, Peter denied the association with Jesus in a stronger way. It says he denied it "with an oath." That would be the equivalent to us saying, "I swear I don't know him." In verse 74 Peter uses the strongest language he could use, which includes wishing oneself to be accursed if he is not being truthful."...or "May I be separated from God forever if I am lying." Immediately following Peter's statement, the cock crowed. Peter remembered Jesus' words and went out from there and wept bitterly.

Luke adds some interesting details to this incident. He states in Luke 22:61-62 that Jesus "turned himself" and "looked upon" Peter. The word for "look" is a word which is intensified by a prefix and can mean "to look in the face", "to fix one's gaze upon". It is safe to say their eyes met. This may have been from quite a distance across the courtyard, but when their eyes met, Peter remembered...then the cock crowed. What did Peter remember? (1) "You will deny me", (2) "I will die", (3) "I will rise", (4) "I have prayed for you", (5) "strengthen your brethren." There is nothing in the text to indicate what kind of look Jesus expressed; however, the fact that their eyes met obviously had a profound effect on Peter.

Jesus' Tone Throughout These Encounters

The tone of Jesus' words was that of *commitment, understanding* and *patience*. This was a difficult time and Jesus bound himself to Peter to give him strength. His words to Peter, "Simon, Simon..." communicated much affection but with just enough distress in the tone to make it solemn.

What Effect it had on Peter

John 21 communicates the final chapter of these events. After His resurrection, Jesus chose to allow Peter to undo his three denials and restored him to a position of leadership in front of his peers...what patience and grace! After Pentecost, Peter would indeed be the rock of the disciples while also becoming the greatest evangelist of the First Century church.

Conclusion

When Jesus was dealing with the disciples, and in particular, Peter, he continually projected unbelievable patience. This trait is most common among the High S profiles.

Notes:

1. Carlo D'Este, Patton A Genius for War, HarperCollins Publishers, New York, NY, ©Copyright 1998, page 586.

2. David Eisenhower, Eisenhower at War 1943-1945, Random House, New York, NY, ©Copyright 1986, page 224.

3. Carlo D'Este, Patton A Genius for War, HarperCollins Publishers, New York, NY, ©Copyright 1998, page 590.

4. Ibid, page 590.

5. Ibid, page 591.

Defining the High & Low Steadiness Continuum

Supportive

Ability to come alongside people in order to accomplish team goals.

Spontaneous

Ability to quickly respond to changing events and issues in order to effectively meet a challenge.

General George S. Patton Jr.

Representative Profile of
General George S. Patton Jr. *

LOW S DISC PROFILE

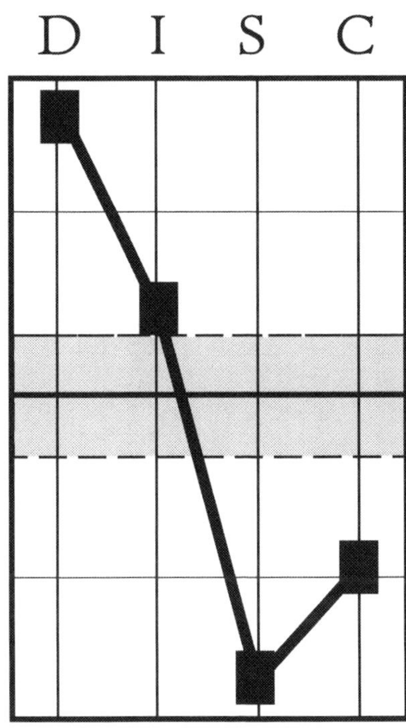

Primary Drive: Strength of character, gets results

Group Giftedness: Acts as a catalyst to carry out difficult assignments

Strength Out of Control: Pushes for action when patience is a better option

Blind Spots: Seeing where their actions contribute to negative consequences[1]

* Based on the historical evidence, the above profile best parallels the behavior style of General Patton but is not intended to be absolute or final.

Notes:

1. Ken Voges & Ron Braund, Understanding How Others Misunderstand You book, ©Copyright 1990, 1995, page 93.

Low S Behavior

Scriptural Case Study
John 2:13-17
Matthew 21:12-14
Mark 11:15-19

General Eisenhower needed a break from the war and was looking forward to attending the wedding of his driver, Sergeant Michael McKeogh. On the previous evening, December 15, 1944, Ike learned that his name was included on a select five-star promotion list to be submitted to the Senate for approval. However, in the back of his mind he remembered that last time he was promoted, the Germans launched a major attack against his forces. He hoped this time it would be different. He was wrong.

At dawn on December 16, two German Panzer armies of twenty-four divisions struck an American corps of three divisions in the Ardennes.[1] Eisenhower was caught by surprise as was everyone else, but he quickly recovered. After assessing the situation, he called a strategy meeting at Verdun on December 19. The room was cold, dismal and depressing which matched the faces of those present. At the meeting was Eisenhower, Tedder, Bedell Smith, Bradley, Devers and Patton along with Maj. Gen. Francis de Guingand, Montgomery's able chief of staff.[2]

As the conference started, Eisenhower opened the meeting with, "The present situation is to be regarded as one of opportunity for us and not of disaster. There will be only cheerful faces at this conference table."[3] True to his impulsive nature, Patton offered an off-color remark about letting the Germans go all the way to Paris and then destroying them. There were forced smiles, but the real issue was how to contain the German forces and when to counterattack.

Eisenhower posed the question to Patton who responded without hesitating that he could attack within 48 hours with three divisions. Patton's confident statement sounded like boastful bravado, which was totally contradictory to the somber mood in the room. It was met with sarcastic laughter. Eisenhower was not amused and said so. The prospect of disengaging three divisions from the line, turning them north, and traveling over 100 miles of icy roads to prepare for a major counter attack in less than seventy-two hours was astonishing, even to a group accustomed to flexibility in their military operations.[4]

But Patton had already worked out three plans in his mind and had discussed them with his staff on the way to the meeting. He had already arranged to use a simple code by phone to indicate to his chief of staff which plan to implement[5] once Eisenhower identified the objective. It was Bastogne. After more than thirty-four years, it was as if destiny had groomed Patton for this single, defining instant in which the fate of the war rested upon the right decisions being made and carried out by the men in that dingy room.[5] Now if the weather would just cooperate.

Patton was a strong believer in prayer. The legend of Patton's famous weather prayer has been erroneously portrayed in the "Patton" film as taking place during the drive to relieve Bastogne.[6] Actually, it occurred in November and was written by Chaplain James O'Nell and printed for the troops for a December distribution. Patton did offer up two prayers during the battle which have been preserved. The first, written on December 23, reads in part:

"Sir, this is Patton talking. The past fourteen days have been straight hell, rain, snow, more rain, more snow---and I am beginning to wonder what's going on in Your headquarters. Whose side are You on anyway? Sir, I have never been an unreasonable man. I am not going to ask You for the impossible...all I request is four days of clear weather...and in exchange for four days of fighting weather, I will deliver You enough Krauts to keep your bookkeepers months behind in their work. Amen."[7]

On December 27, there was another Patton address to God: "Sir, this is Patton again, and I beg to report complete progress. Sir, it seems to me that You have been much better informed about the situation than I was, because it was that awful weather which I cursed so much which made it possible for the German army to commit suicide. That, Sir, was a brilliant military move, and I bow humbly to a supreme military genius."[8]

Although some individuals might feel the prayers inappropriate or mocking God, the tone is fairly accurate of how High D, Low S individuals think. Furthermore, when it came to God, Patton was always dead earnest.[9] Patton's leadership ensured victory in what is called the Battle of the Bulge. During the operation, the Third Army moved farther and faster and engaged more divisions in less time than any other army in the history of the United States.[10]

Later in the war, Third Army would be the instrument in liberating various concentration camps. Patton was utterly incensed and disgusted with what he saw. As an expression of his fury over Nazi bestiality, at Ohrdruf and other camps, Patton aggressively compelled the local townspeople to dig graves and bury the corpses of the dead.[11] Patton also informed Eisenhower who deliberately inspected each camp. Eisenhower did this, according to his words, in order "to be in position to give firsthand evidence of these things if ever, in the future, there develops a tendency to charge these allegations merely as 'propaganda'.[12] Eisenhower and Patton teamed together to insure that others personally witnessed this horrific act of the Nazis. Soldiers, politicians and civilians were paraded through the camps so that the holocaust would never be forgotten.

Today, the government of Bavaria maintains a memorial and museum on the site of one of the concentration camps near the town of Dachau. In front of the International Memorial is a sign translated in five languages which reads: "Never again!"

Genesis 21:8-14
[Sarah & Abraham]

"...Sarah saw that the son whom Hagar the Egyptian had borne to Abraham was mocking and she said to Abraham, 'Get rid of that slave woman and her son, for the slave woman's son will never share in the inheritance with my son Isaac.' "

"The matter distressed Abraham greatly because it concerned his son. But God said to him, 'Do not be so distressed about the boy and your maidservant. Listen to whatever Sarah tells you, because it is through Isaac that your offspring will be reckoned."

Whereas a High S desires structure and order, a Low S profile desires variety and change. In addition, a Low S is skilled in creatively adapting to the needs of a situation whereas the High S will tend to respond to the same situation in a more traditional manner. Low S profiles spontaneously act and react in bringing about change. They also tend to be the first in actively confronting issues.

> Word Pictures - decisive, doer, determined, spontaneous, action-oriented, aggressive in challenging activities that go against their value system.

> What the Low S Style Produces in Others - a sense of urgency, awareness that a serious problem exists and needs to be corrected immediately.

Sarah's Low Steadiness Leadership Style

The real gift of the Low S behavior is the ability to quickly respond to changing events and issues in order to effectively meet a challenge. It is the ability to be spontaneous. It does not mean that the quick response is always the right response, but often it is.

This is the case in the situation in Genesis 21, where a problem arose between Sarah's stepson, Ishmael, and her own son, Isaac. There is, however, much background to this incident that sheds light on the actions of both Sarah and Abraham.

In Chapter 16, we find Sarah and Abraham both getting old and Sarah had not been able to conceive and bear a child. Sarah therefore suggests that Abraham use Sarah's servant, Hagar, as a surrogate, so that they can have a child. This was done, but after Hagar conceived, she looked down on Sarah. Sarah then began to treat Hagar harshly and Hagar fled. An angel appeared to Hagar and told her to return to Sarah and submit to her authority. It was in those circumstances that Ishmael was born. Thirteen years later, God appeared to Abraham and said that Sarah would conceive her own son.

Chapter 21 begins with the birth of Isaac. His name means "laughter" which seems significant since both Sarah and Abraham laughed at the idea that they could bear a son in their old age. Sarah says the name indicates that "everyone will laugh with me (in happiness)." (v.6) This name seems ironically significant in the upcoming turmoil. A feast for Isaac's weaning (2-3 years old) was being held, and at this feast in honor of Isaac, Ishmael "mocked" Isaac. (v. 8) The word "mocked" comes from the same root as the name Isaac, only it is an intensified form. Ishmael was persecuting Isaac, the son of promise, and Sarah didn't like it. She told Abraham to "drive them out" because Ishmael was not going to be an heir with Isaac.

Now this troubled Abraham (v. 11) because he loved both of his sons and wanted Ishmael to inherit something. Sarah understood that Isaac was in the promised line of inheritance, not Ishmael, but Abraham was balking. God then told Abraham, "listen to Sarah. . . through Isaac your descendants will be named." God then promised Abraham that Ishmael would also be the head of a great nation. So Abraham complied and sent Hagar and Ishmael out of the home.

Sarah responded quickly to a potentially "ugly" situation and her instincts were confirmed by God to be correct. Isaac was in the promised line of Abraham's descendants and Ishmael was the beginning of the Arab nations.

Jesus' Low Steadiness Leadership Style

The perceived behavior of Jesus is generally one of patience, grace and forgiveness. However, when He encountered the Jewish religious institution and its traditions, Jesus' behavior became very aggressive and confrontational. Two incidents come to mind and both involve the temple.

First Cleansing the Temple: John 2:13-17

And the Passover of the Jews was at hand, and Jesus went up to Jerusalem.

And He found in the temple those who were selling oxen and sheep and the money changers seated.

And He made a scourge of cords, and drove them all out of the temple, with the sheep and the oxen; and

He poured out the coins of the money changers, and overturned their tables;

And to those who were selling the doves He said, 'take these things away; stop making My Fathers's house a house of merchandise.'

Expression of Support through Action

In the Lord's actions in the Temple court, we see the fulfillment of Mal. 3:1-3 and Psalm 69:9. The corruption that had originated as a convenience to pilgrims who came to the Passover celebration had developed into a noisy, smelly bazaar. The changing of foreign coins into Jewish coinage for the Temple tax and the purchasing of animals for the sacrifices had all crept into the outer court of the Temple. This became a lucrative market operated for the profit of the family of the high priest.

This noisy, smelly, exorbitant market place defiled the Temple. The Lord wanted to restore the purity of purpose for which the Temple existed, or at least point out, in a very vivid way, the extent of the defilement. The defilement didn't come so much from what they were doing as from where they were doing it.

Second Cleansing of the Temple - Matthew 21:12-13

And Jesus entered the temple and cast out all those who were buying and selling in the temple, and he overturned the tables of the money changers and the seats of those who were selling doves

And He said to them, 'It is written, 'MY HOUSE SHALL BE CALLED A HOUSE OF PRAYER'; but you are making it a robber's den.'

In the second cleansing of the Temple, after His Triumphal Entry into Jerusalem, Jesus points to additional offenses that were going on in the Temple bazaar. In quoting parts of Isaiah 56:7 and Jeremiah 7:11, Jesus points out the irony of what the Temple should be, and what it had become. While one purpose of the Temple was to be a house of prayer for all people, the religious leaders had let it become a place to cheat pilgrims by an exorbitant exchange rate of money and overpriced animals for sacrifice. These defilements, which God denounced in Old Testament times, had returned to the Temple in even more outrageous forms.

In Mark 11, the author adds a few details that Matthew doesn't mention. Verse 16 states that Jesus would not permit anyone to carry goods through the Temple. People used the Temple mount as a shortcut to go from the old city to the Mount of Olives. Using the Temple
complex in this way was another defilement of the Temple for common purpose.

Jesus' Tone Throughout the Encounters

The Lord's actions and words were that of judgement and disgust. He was certainly confrontational and aggressive in His cleansing of the Temple court. While His actions on both occasions appear to be spontaneous, the Lord was clearly incensed by the gross commercialism taking place in the courts of the Temple. Those sights and sounds of the bazaar in God's holy house of worship and prayer simply demanded a response--and He gave them one!

The Response of the People

Mark mentions that the leaders were plotting to kill Jesus because the people were wowed by his teachings. The word translated "astonished" is a very strong Greek word, which means to strike out of ones senses. The people were almost beside themselves because of the difference between Jesus' teachings and that of the Jewish religious leaders.

In Matthew's account, the response of the people was to come to Him while He was still in the Temple and to ask for healing, which he did. In the second cleansing, the people were identifying Him as the Messiah, and flocking to Him, which made the leaders' indignant.

John states that the people asked for a sign of His authority for doing what He had just done in the Temple. They recognized this as an act of authority and were wanting some kind of a divine sign to authenticate what He believed to have been His source of power and authority.

Conclusion

In the S continuum, both styles solve problems

differently. The High Steadiness leadership style tends to seek consensus and is more deliberate and patient while the Low Steadiness is more independent and spontaneous. In the examples of Eisenhower and Patton, both of their expressions of support in solving problems were very different and both correctly met the need. Eisenhower's major flaw was his inability to resist being influenced by other views. It was said of Ike, his plan often reflected the last person he talked to. Patton's flaws were numerous but often centered around his impetuous nature.

Jesus showed both styles depending on the needs of the situation. With Peter and the disciples, who were naive but sought God's righteousness, Jesus tended to be affirming and patient. Behaviorally, this best reflects the traits of a High Steadiness leadership style. With self-righteous and self-confident religious leaders and their traditions and activities, He tended to be aggressive and reactive. Regarding issues concerning commercializing the activities in and around the Temple, He was very impatient and confrontational. The latter behavior best reflects the traits of a Low Steadiness leadership style.

Notes:

1. Stephen Ambrose, The Supreme Commander, The War Years of Dwight D. Eisenhower, University Press, Jackson Mississippi, ©Copyright 1970, page 553.

2. Carol D'Este, Patton A Genius for War, HarperCollins Publishers , New York, NY, ©Copyright 1995, page 679.

3. Dwight D. Eisenhower, Crusade in Europe, DoubleDay & Company, Inc., Garden City New York, ©Copyright 1949 page 350.

4. Carol D'Este, Patton, A Genius for War, HarperCollins Publishers , New York, NY, ©Copyright 1995, page 680.

5. Martin Blumenson, Patton, The Man Behind the Legend, 1885-1945, Quill, William Marrow, New York. NY, ©Copyright 1985, page 251.

6. Carol D'Este, Patton, A Genius for War, HarperCollins Publishers , New York, NY, ©Copyright 1995, page 685.

7. Ibid, page 686.

8. Ibid, page 687.

9. Ibid, page 689.

10. Ibid, page 702.

11. Ibid, page 720.

12. Stephen Ambrose, The Supreme Commander, The War Years of Dwight D. Eisenhower, University Press, Jackson Mississippi, © Copyright 1970, page 659.

Defining the Cautious Continuum

Procedure

Having the ability to set in motion a particular course of action designed to accomplish specific results.

Restraint

Having the ability to hold back feelings, comments and retaliatory actions so as not to endanger plans or persons.

General Omar N. Bradley

Representative Profile of
General Omar N. Bradley *

HIGH C DISC PROFILE

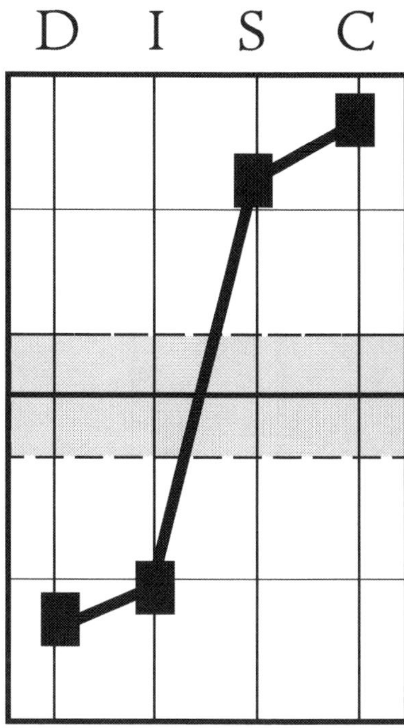

Primary Drive: Critical thinking, being cooperative, validating data

Personal Giftedness: Team player, good at follow-through, commitment to quality and order

Group Giftedness: Adapting to those in authority[1]

Instinctive Fears: Criticism directed toward them[2]

* Based on the historical evidence, the above profile best parallels the behavior style of General Bradley but is not intended to be absolute or final.

Notes:

1. Ken Voges & Ron Braund, Understanding How Others Misunderstand You book, ©Copyright 1990, 1995 page 224.

2. Ken Voges & Ron Braund, Understanding How Others Misunderstand You workbook, ©Copyright 1990, 1999 page 90.

High C Behavior

Scriptural Case Study
Exodus 32

General Omar Bradley was considered by many to have been the greatest military strategist of WWII. Although extremely quiet, calm and mild-mannered, Bradley had impressed Eisenhower with his high intelligence, good judgement, and strength of character.[1] Bradley handled his army commanders with respect, common sense and great tactical skill. Furthermore, his complete loyalty and trust in Eisenhower's leadership made him an ideal subordinate and one in whom Ike had great confidence.[2] Consequently, Eisenhower constantly sought Bradley's council.

During the critical meeting at Verdun on December 19, 1944 Eisenhower was even more impressed with Bradley on how he "kept his head" in lieu of the potential disaster that was confronting them. Bradley, senior commander, quietly allowed Patton to take the lead in outlining how to defend and counterattack the German offensive. The key to victory was whether Patton could quickly relieve the 101st Airborne unit which was holding the critical crossroads at Bastogne. Patton's bravado was inspiring but Ike was counting on Bradley's quiet, tactful support.

True to form, the next day, December 20, Patton contemplated ceding Bastogne to the Germans, but Bradley disagreed and a plan was formulated for its relief. Knowing the southern counterattack was his number one priority, Bradley situated his headquarters near Patton's army. However, because Bradley was situated on the southern edge of the bulge, Eisenhower felt that temporary command of the northern sector needed to be transferred to British General Bernard Montgomery. This included Bradley's First and Ninth Armies.

Bradley protested this move, voicing concern that the change-over would discredit the American command. Ike naively dismissed Bradley's concerns and assured him that nothing of the kind would happen and that the change would indeed be temporary. However, Montgomery did use the opportunity to revive his demands to gain operational control over all armies in the theatre and to put pressure on Eisenhower to give him that authority.

In the meantime, Bradley actively went about his business supporting Patton's efforts to rescue the embattled troops in Bastogne. Patton did indeed engage the Germans on the 23rd and was set to link up with the 101st the day after Christmas. Patton and Bradley were confident the Germans had achieved their high water mark and the link-up would indeed be the beginning of the end of the battle.

Bradley received word that Montgomery desired a conference on December 25 to discuss coordinating their efforts. Bradley flew to Montgomery's headquarters expecting Montgomery to announce a northern attack by the First Army to support Patton's attack from the south. Instead, Bradley had to endure an insulting lecture on the shortcomings of the American broad front strategy. Monty suggested that the best thing he, Bradley, could do was to order a retreat, regroup and attack in three months.

In a letter to one of his political allies, Montgomery thought Bradley looked thin and worn and ill at ease, and added, incorrectly, that the American had agreed with everything he had said. He went on patronizingly: 'Poor chap, he is such a decent fellow and the whole thing is a bitter pill for him."[4]

The truth is, Bradley silently disagreed with every word Monty uttered. He wrote, "Never in my life had I been so enraged and so utterly exasperated. It required every fiber of my strength to restrain myself from an insulting outburst. Somehow I remained silent, seething inside, nodding as Monty imperiously rattled on. I admitted to nothing. ... I kept my counsel."[5] Futhermore, Bradley stayed with his plan in supporting Third Army's aggressive efforts. The next day, Patton's 4th Armored Division relieved Bastogne, thus ending the first phase of one of the most dramatic battles of the war.

Thanks to Bradley's planning and restraint, Eisenhower's support and Patton's grit, their efforts resulted in victory. Later, in a speech before the House of Commons, Churchill would agree.

Exodus 32:1-35
[Moses, Aaron & God]

"Moses saw that people were running wild and that Aaron had let them get out of control... So he stood at the entrance to the camp and said,'Whoever is for the Lord, come to me.' And all the Levites rallied to him."

"The next day Moses said to the people, 'You have committed a great sin. But now I will go up to the Lord; perhaps I can make atonement for your sins.'

So Moses went back to the Lord."

High C tendencies are characteristic of a leader who is committed to accuracy and excellence in quality control. Typically, once a High C takes ownership of a plan of action, compliance is assured down to the smallest detail.

> Word Pictures - cautious, calculating, courteous, compentent, model of diplomacy and restraint, committed and loyal and to an agreed upon plan down to the last item.

> What the High C Style Produces in Others - a model of consistency to be measured by a total commitment to excellence.

Moses' Conscientious Leadership Style

The High C leadership style, as displayed by Moses, has the ability to set in motion a particular course of action designed to accomplish specific results. The specific plan that Moses had signed on to was the leading of the Children of Israel out of Egypt and into the promised land. The fact that Moses had committed to this plan doesn't mean that it came easily to him. High C behavior tends to be very unsure of new things and very cautious. The early chapters of Exodus outline Moses' fears and arguments which God answered before Moses would agree to the plan. In Ex. 4:18 we read, "Then Moses departed and returned to Jethro, his father-in-law, and said to him, 'Please, let me go, that I may return to my brethren. . .'" Moses had committed himself to God's plan and he would follow it through.

The commitment of Moses to follow the original plan can be seen in his determination to reach the desired conclusion. In Exodus 32:7-10, God confronts Moses concerning the sin of the people. God outlines their sin and then says, "Let me alone, that my anger may burn against them, and that I may destroy them; and I will make of you a great nation."

The response of Moses was a logical argument as to why God should not do what He had just said. It is logical to continue the plan, because: (1) You are the one who brought them out of the land of Egypt (v. 11); and (2) Your reputation is at stake because the Egyptians will say You brought them out of Egypt just to kill them (v. 12); and (3) You made promises to Abraham, Isaac and Israel that You must fulfill. To Moses, it was only logical to continue the plan that God had initiated and he had signed on to.

It says in verse 14 that "God changed His mind." A better translation of that phrase might be, "God relented or restrained from the harm He said He would do to His people." Augustine says, "An unexpected change in the things which God has put in His own power is called 'repentance'." The Hebrew word here gives the idea of relief from some planned or undesirable course of action. God didn't "change His mind," He embarked on a different course of action.

Moses then went down the mountain and got the attention of the people. He shattered the tablets of the Law (v. 19), destroyed the golden calf in a ceremony that the Israelites would not forget (v. 20), had 3,000 of the people slain (vs. 25-28), and had the remaining Israelites dedicate themselves again to following God (v. 29). Moses then said he would try to intercede for them with God, and went back up the mountain (v. 30).

When Moses returned to the presence of God, he admitted the great sin that the people had done. Then Moses asked God to forgive them, and if He couldn't forgive them, to take Moses' life. (vs. 31-32) The phrase "blot me out from the book which Thou hast written" is not a reference to eternal death, but to physical death. In essence, Moses said, "let's stick with the original plan, or I don't want to be involved, and You can kill me now." He didn't want to be associated with a rebellious, unforgiven people, and would rather suffer a premature physical death. The book Moses was referring to was probably the census of God's people, Israel.

God, in reality, rejected Moses' alternative on both counts. He was not going to take Moses' life, and He was not going to completely forgive the people for their sin. Those who sinned, would die when God chose to use His physical judgment. However, He was not going to do away with the nation, and told Moses to take those who were left and continue the original plan (v. 34).

Jesus' Conscienteous Leadership Style

In the context of the passages below, Jesus was about to be arrested by a mob led by Judas. The intent was to take Him to the High Priest for trial.

Expression of Restraint in Order to Complete a Plan

And Jesus said to him [Judas], "Friend, do what you have come for." Then they came and laid hands on Jesus and seized Him.

And behold, one of those who were with Jesus [Peter] reached and drew out his sword, and struck the slave of the high priest and cut off his ear.

But Jesus answered and said, "Stop! No more of this." And He touched his ear and healed him.

Then Jesus said to him, "Put your sword back into its place; for all those who take up the sword shall perish by the sword."

When Peter started swinging his sword, Jesus stopped him. He rebuked Peter and warned him that those who take up the sword will reap the consequences. Jesus then proceeded to clarify His mission.

"Or do you think that I cannot appeal to My Father, and He will at once put at My disposal more than twelve legions of angels?

How then shall the Scriptures be fulfilled, that it must happen this way."

At the time Jesus said to the multitudes, "Have you come out with swords and clubs to arrest Me as though I were a robber? Every day I used to sit in the temple teaching and you did not seize Me.

But all this has taken place that the Scriptures of the prophets may be fulfilled." Then all the disciples left Him and fled."

If it was Jesus' desire to be rescued, He instantly had available 12 legions of angels [approximately 36,000 to 72,000 in number] but that was not the plan.

Jesus clarified the events by restating that these things <u>must happen</u> for Scripture to be fulfilled. In verse 56, He repeats this thought to the crowd by saying, "All this has taken place to fulfill the Prophets..." What incredible restraint He displayed in order that the Scripture would be fulfilled!

During the trial, false testimony was given.

"This man stated, I am able to destroy the temple of God and to rebuild it in three days."

And the high priest stood up and said to Him, "Do You make no answer? What is it that these men are testifying against You?"

But Jesus kept silent. And the high priest said to

Him, "I adjure You by the living God, that You tell us whether You are the Christ, the Son of God."

In verses 61-63, the charge against Jesus was a misinterpretation of what He said about His own body – but He didn't answer the charge. The imperfect tense signifies that He continued to keep silent during the series of accusations. The word "adjure" means to put someone under oath using divine names and titles which renders the oath binding.

[Then] "Jesus said to him, 'You have said it yourself; nevertheless I tell you, hereafter you shall see the Son of Man sitting at the right hand of power, and coming on the clouds of heaven.'"

Jesus said "You are the one who said it." Then Jesus identifies with the prophecies of Psalm 110 and Daniel 7:13.

The trial then adjourned to Pilate, the Roman governor, where a similar question would be asked.

"Now Jesus stood before the governor, and the governor questioned Him, saying, 'Are You the King of the Jews?' and Jesus said to him, 'It is as you say.'"

The expression of Jesus "<u>You</u> are saying it." is meant to affirm the accusation. It is not intended to suggest that it was only the accuser's statement. What this meant to Pilate was that Jesus was the leader of the resistance to Rome.

"And while He was being accused by the chief priests and elders, He made no answer."

Matthew 26:50-56, Luke 22:51

Jesus' Tone Throughout the Encounters

The Lord continued to display incredible restraint. Jesus only affirmed their statements as to who He was. What makes His behavior so remarkable is He had the power and the resources to truly ruin their day but He chose not to. His total commitment was to fulfill the Father's plan of salvation for us without compromising His identity by denying it.

The Response of the People

The high priest, the council and Pilate never got it. They remained totally threatened and decided that the solution to the problem was to kill Him...which was the Father's plan.

Conclusion

Facing certain death, Jesus chose to endure the betrayal, arrest, trial and the agony of the cross so that the redemption of man would be completed. In human terms, His incredible restraint could best be characterized as High C behavior.

Notes:

1. Edgar F. Puryear, Jr., 19 Stars, Presido Press, Novato, CA, ©Copyright 1971 page 218.

2. Steven Ambrose, The Supreme Commander, University Press of Mississippi, Jackson, Mississippi, ©Copyright 1970 page 622.

3. David Eisenhower, Eisenhower at War 1943-1945, Random House, New York, NY, ©Copyright 1986, page 586.

4. Richard Lamb, Montgomery in 1943-1945, Buchan & Enright Publishers, London, England, ©Copyright 1983, page 316.

5. Omar N. Bradley and Clay Blair, A General's Life, An Autobiography by General of the Army Omar N Bradley, Simon and Schuster, New York, NY, ©Copyright 1983 page 370.

Defining the High & Low Conscientious Continuum

Facts

Ability to non-emotionally remember and recall detailed information critical to solving an issue.

Feelings

Ability to express an emotion so that others understand the critical nature of an issue.

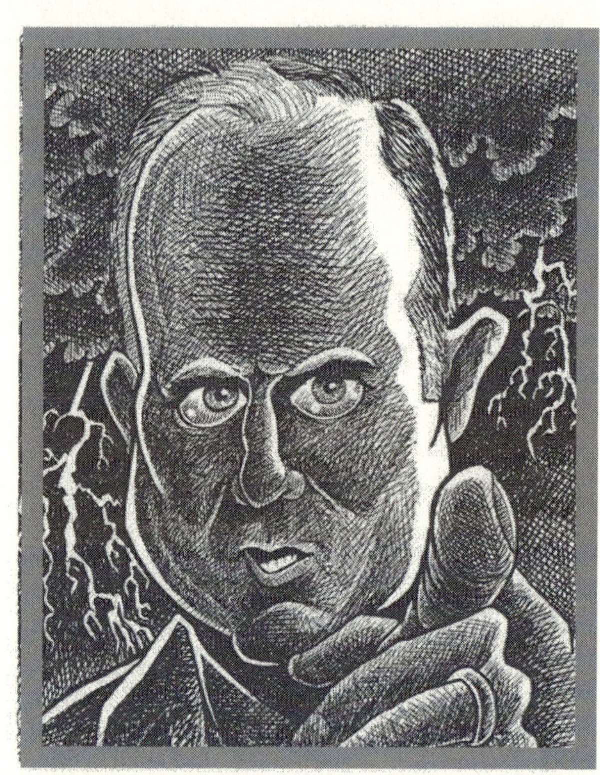

General H. Norman Schwarzkophf

Representative Profile of
General H. Norman Schwarzkophf.*

Low C DISC PROFILE

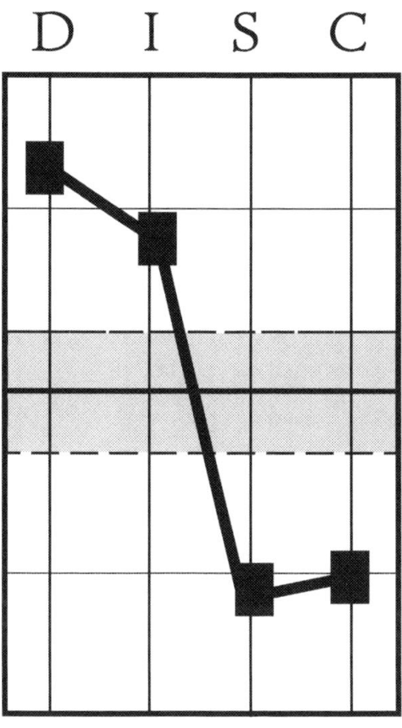

Primary Drive: Strength of character

Personal Giftedness: Taking charge, acting as a catalyst to carrying out difficult assignments

Instinctive Fears: Slowness, especially in seeing a task or goal accomplished

Blind Spots: Seeing where their aggressive actions contribute to negative consequences [1]

* Based on the historical evidence, the above profile best parallels the behavior style of General Schwarzkophf but is not intended to be absolute or final.

Notes:

1. Ken Voges & Ron Braund, Understanding How Others Misunderstand You workbook, ©Copyright 1999, page 54.

Low C Behavior

Scriptural Case Studies
Acts 7: 1-60
Matthew 23:1-36

On February 27, 1991 at 9:00 p.m., General Norman Schwarzkophf walked into the briefing room at the Hyatt Regency Hotel in Riyadh [Saudi Arabia] to deliver his report to the nation.[1] The ground war had gone extremely well and he was about to conduct the "mother of all briefings" before reporters and live television. Through use of various charts, Schwarzkophf dramatically highlighted how victory was achieved by the ground assault into Kuwait, and he then opened the briefing to questions from the reporters and invited guests.

One reporter asked, "Can I ask you two questions: Did you think it would be such an easy cake walk as it seemed, and what are your impressions of Saddam Hussein as a military strategist?"[2]

Schwarzkophf answered with a "Hah!" which drew a spontaneous laugh from the audience.

Schwarzkophf then defended the preparation of his battle plans which included a six-week supply of materials and acknowledged he didn't expect the victory to be achieved that quickly. He then leaned onto the podium and glared directly at the reporter with an intense look and emotionally expressed what he thought of Saddam Hussein.

Dripping with sarcasm, Schwarzkophf stated the following thoughts as the camera zoomed in on his face: "Concerning Saddam Hussein as a great military strategist, he is neither a military strategist, nor is he schooled in the operational arts [of war], nor is he a tactician, nor is he a general, nor is he a soldier. Other than that he's a great military man, I want you to know that." His answer drew an even greater round of laughter and he quickly went to the next question. It was obvious Schwarzkophf was extremely emotional about the subject of Hussein's leadership style and vented nothing but contempt for what the man stood for.

To further understand Schwarzkophf's answer, one must understand his value system and training. First and foremost, Schwarzkophf genuinely loved his troops. Their safety and ultimate survival was one of his chief passions.[3] In contrast, Saddam Hussein had a totally opposite focus. Convinced that Americans would not tolerate heavy casualties, the Iraqis' hope had been to force a stalemate on the battlefield in which the Americans took steady losses, which would stir up political opposition to the war at home.[4] He didn't really care how many troops he lost so long as he achieved his goal of a negotiated peace, leaving him in control of Kuwait and its oil.

Regarding the science of operational arts, Schwarzkophf and the US military were schooled in tactics of how to coordinate their efforts. In essence, successful battles and engagements had to be linked together in both time and space in the design of a campaign to achieve a larger operational objective. Achievement of that operational objective would lead to gaining the overall theater strategic objective and victory.[5] In Schwarzkophf's opinion, Saddam didn't have a clue in this arena.

Regarding being a soldier, a leader should be a part of the troops' lives. During Christmas, Schwarzkophf mingled with his officers and enlisted men on duty wishing them a Merry Christmas and thanking them for serving their country. In the course of four hours standing in mess lines, he had shaken four thousand hands. Schwarzkophf commented, "As had happened many times before in my Army career, I'd set out to make my troops feel good, and they responded by making me feel good."[6] In contrast, Saddam remained aloof and in total control. If he felt threatened by one of his officers, soldiers or officials, the individual would simply disappear.

It was obvious to all who attended the briefing that Schwarzkophf viewed Hussein in total contempt and disgust. Their value systems were on opposite ends of the scale, particularly as it applied to the value of the life of human beings. The emotions and feelings expressed by Schwarzkophf told the whole story and the television cameras captured it for all posterity.

Acts 7:51-60
[Stephen & the Sanhedrin]

"You stiff-necked people with uncircumcised hearts and ears! You are just like your fathers You always resist the Holy Spirit! Was there ever a prophet your fathers did not persecute? They even killed those who predicted the coming of the Righteous One. And now you have betrayed and murdered him---you who have received the law that was put into effect through angels but have not obeyed it."

"When they heard this, they were furious and gnashed their teeth at him...covered their ears and yelled at the top of their voices, they all rushed at him, dragged him out of the city and began to stone him."

Whereas a High C desires procedures and order, a Low C profile prefers a spontaneous approach. In addition, a Low C is skilled in knowing when to challenge the status quo.

> Word Pictures - interactive, involved in bringing about change, rebellious, defiant, sarcastic toward individuals they perceive to be hypocritical, have a tendency to be a lightning rod for challenging perceived hypocrisy.

> What Low C Style Produces in Others - Others are influenced to rally in support of challenging the system; unfortuately, those who are attacked tend to counterattack; war often ensues.

Stephen's Low Consceientious Leadership Style

The Low C personality has the ability to express an emotion so that others understand the critical nature of an issue. Stephen certainly got the attention of the religious leaders of Israel when he preached to them before the Council of the Sanhedrin.

The background to Stephen's sermon to the council is found in chapter six of the book of Acts. It says that many, even priests, were coming to Christ in faith (v. 7). Then some from the Synagogue of Freedmen began to argue with Stephen about his teaching, but couldn't prevail in their arguments (v.9). So they put some people up to lying about what Stephen said, and had Stephen dragged before the council. (11-12) Then these false accusations were made of Stephen, and (7:1) the council asked Stephen if these charges were true.

Stephen then began to give them a summary of the history of Israel, highlighting all the important points (vs. 2-38). When Stephen got to the incident of the Golden Calf, he pointed out the disobedience of their forefathers, and how it resulted in the 40 years in the wilderness. (v. 39ff)

Stephen then began to push their emotional buttons. He said (v. 51), "You men are stiff necked and uncircumcised of heart." He added that they were always resisting the Holy Spirit, just as their fathers had done. Then he stated that their fathers persecuted all the prophets and the messengers who were sent to announce the coming of the "Righteous One." Stephen then got personal and said that they had become the betrayers and murderers of that "Righteous One." (v. 52) On top of that, Stephen said, they received the Law, ordained by angels, but did not keep it! (v. 53)

The response of the people was predictable. They were cut to the quick and began gnashing their teeth at him. It means to grind the teeth together loudly, in a show of strong anguish and disapproval.

But Stephen was not intimidated by their actions. He simply looked up into heaven (being full of the Holy Spirit), and saw the glory of God, and Jesus standing at the right hand of God. Stephen stated, "Behold I see the heavens opened up and the Son of Man standing at the right hand of God." Now this was a clincher of a statement for three reasons: (1) It repeats the claim that Jesus made at His trial when He was accused of blasphemy; (2) The term "Son of Man" is definitely a messianic term from Daniel 7:13-14, and Jesus used the term to refer to Himself in this way; (3) This verse, in combining references to Daniel 7and Psalm 110:1, both messianic passages, makes a special emphasis on the deity and Sonship of Christ.

This was more than the people could take... they cried out, covered their ears, pounced upon him and drove him out of the city and stoned him to death. (Verse 58 shows that the necessary witnesses were present, making this a legal response of the council to religious blasphemy.)

Stephen's words while he was being stoned had to cut them even deeper. He asked Jesus to receive his spirit and asked that this sin not be held against them.

Stephen certainly got their attention. He pushed every emotional button these council members had and his emotional speech brought them to the clear realization of his message--Jesus is the Messiah and you killed Him!

Jesus' Low Conscientious Leadership Style

Based on their interpretation of the Law, the scribes and Pharisees continually challenged Jesus. From their perspective, Jesus and His disciples flagrantly violated specific rules or laws. They felt compelled to bring these indiscretions to His attention. In Matthew 23:1-36, Jesus turned the table on them and communicated a seething criticism on how they had turned the Mosaic system into an empty ritual of hypocrisy.

Low C - Criticism Based on Emotion

First, in verses 1-12 , Jesus said, "they tell you, do and observe, but do not do according to their deeds; for they say things and do not do them...they widen the fringe on their hem and tassels on their robes to be more noticeable. . .love the place of honor at banquets ...and respectful greetings... and being called by men...Rabbi."

Their pride and hypocrisy ran full circle. They had no problem telling others what to do but had no intention of applying their rules and traditions to themselves. Their physical appearance communicated their importance in the community and demanded honor among men.

In verses 13-33, Jesus gave a series of strong condemnations based on the hypocrisy of their lives.
Each started out with "Woe to you, Scribes and Phari-

sees, hypocrites. . ." The word "woe" means a judgmental insertion and "hypocrites" means pretenders, play actors. In essence, Jesus was warning and passing judgment on them for being religious pretenders in a system that the Father set up as sacred. Since He represented the Father, He was taking their offensiveness against the Father personally.

Jesus continued the list of offenses:

v. 13 "You shut off the kingdom of heaven from men...

v. 14 You devour widows' houses, even while for a pretense you make long prayers...

v.15 You make a convert, then corrupt him even worse than you are!

v. 16 You are blind guides - you materialize the Temple of God.

v.23 You tithe even on little things, but don't show mercy and justice!

v.25 You clean your outside appearance, but are dirty on the inside.

v.27 You look like a beautiful whitewashed tomb, but inside are dead men's bones.

> v.29 You honor the Prophets that your fathers killed – but you fill up the measure of guilt of your fathers."

In verse 33, Jesus interjects the strongest language yet – "You serpents, you brood of vipers, how shall you escape the sentence of Hell?"

In verses 34-35, Jesus then cast judgment on them.

> "I am sending Prophets & wise men, whom you will kill and crucify...You are guilty of all the innocent blood shed from Abel to Zechariah."

To say Jesus did not like what they were doing is a gross understatement.

Jesus' Tone in Dealing With the Pharisees

The Lord's tone was scalding, His words searing and His conclusion devastating. Nowhere in the Scriptures do you find more condemning emotion then the verse focusing on the actions of the religious leaders.

The Response of the People and Pharisees

As a result of Jesus' teaching and miracles many of the people believed in Him. But, the Chief Priests and Pharisees became threatened by Him and looked for an opportunity to kill Him. Of course, that was God's plan.

Conclusion

In the High C continuum, each leadership style communicates emotions differently. The High C will tend to outwardly control emotion, whereas the Low C tends to visibly express emotion. In the examples of Bradley, Moses, Schwarzkophf and Stephen, all expressed their feelings differently. Bradley and Moses were extremely restrained, whereas Schwarzkophf and Stephen were very intense and expressive. Each was very effective in their given situation. However, Bradley's flaw was that his repressed anger later boiled over against Eisenhower. He never forgave Ike for making the changes which affected his command. Moses too would lash out in anger against the people in Numbers 20. His disobedient actions against the Lord would prevent him from entering the promise land. Schwarzkophf's nickname, "Stormin' Norman" needs no further comment. Stephen's intense, concluding statements in Acts 7 resulted in being stoned to death.

Again, Jesus' expression of feelings was always in balance. His restraint at His arrest and trial was calculated and necessary so that the prophecy might be fulfilled. Behaviorally, this best parallels the High C traits. His passionate and emotional comments against the religious leaders and their traditions was justified. Without a doubt, His greatest criticism was against these leaders, particularly the Pharisees, the self-proclaimed scholars and protectors of the Jewish law. I believe, Jesus' unrelenting, emotional attacks best fit the behavioral traits of a Low C blended with a High D profile.

Notes:

1. Michale R. Gordon and General Bernard E. Trainor, The Generals' War, Little, Brown & Company, New York, NY, ©Copyright 1995, page 416.

2. ABC News, Schwarzkophf, How the War was Won (The Briefing), MPI, Home Video, ©Copyright 1991.

3. Tom Clancy with General Chuck Horner, Every Man a Tiger, G.P. Putnam's Sons, New York, NY, ©Copyright 1999, page 275.

4. Michale R. Gordon and Gerneral Bernard E. Trainor, The Generals' War, Little, Brown & Company, New York, NY, ©Copyright 1995, page 269.

5. Tom Clancy with General Fred Franks, Into the Storm, Berkley Books, New York, NY, ©Copyright 1997, page 139.

6. General H. Norman Schwarzkopf, It Does't Take a Hero, Bantam Books, New York, NY, ©Copyright 1992, page 399.

Part 2

The Transitional Leadership Styles of Jesus

"A servant leader serves the mission and leads by serving those on mission with him."

Gene Wilkes
Jesus on Leadership

The Transitional Leadership Styles of Jesus

Part 2

We have covered the eight different DISC continuums by looking at examples of both famous military and political figures and Jesus projecting specific behavioral styles to meet specific needs in a given situation. It should be clear that no one temperament is superior for leadership. In Gene Wilkes' fine book, Jesus on Leadership, he relates God's perspective on the subject. "God didn't go looking for leaders. God looked for obedient people who He then formed into leaders."[1]

When God has a mission He wants accomplished, the limitations of the temperaments do not matter to Him. What does matter to the Father is availability, flexibility and obedience. The Biblical case studies seem to show that God always provides additional resources to support areas of limitations in skills. The team of Moses and Aaron is a classic example. One of Moses' High C excuses in being God's spokesman before Pharaoh was that he was slow of tongue. The statement was true; however, the Lord already had the solution: Moses' brother

Aaron, the High I, was gifted in that area. Neither liked playing the heavy and God took that role.

A truly effective leader has the ability to transition one's style to meet different needs in the same situation. What this means is that a similar event involving different people may require different styles. As an example, should a family or community experience the death of a loved one, each grieving individual may need comfort expressed with a different tone, a different nonverbal action or different words. The challenge is knowing which style to use in comforting each individual person while always being aware of the needs of the entire group. Such effectiveness requires insightful sensitivity, knowledge, experience, maturity and openess to God's leadership. Without a doubt, Jesus is the model from which we can develop these skills.

To understand this concept, we will, again, look at parallel case studies involving people caught up in highly emotional situations, demanding different but appropriate responses. As before, comparisons and conclusions will be drawn between a modern-day example and situations involving Christ. Comparisons will be drawn; but a special focus will be on the behavior of Jesus as He changes styles. The case studies will show a transitional behavioral response meeting different needs and agendas all at the same time.

Notes:

Gene Wilkes, Jesus on Leadership, Tyndale House Publishers, Inc. Wheaton, IL, ©Copyright 1999, page 145.

Case Studies of the Transitional Leadership Styles of Jesus

Scripture Study
John 11:1-37

A number of years ago, my pastor, Roger Raymer, asked if I, Ken, would serve as interim Christian Education Director until the church leadership could sort out what they wanted to do with the position. I had held several lay positions in the church but this would be my first opportunity to actually serve as a staff member. Roger mentioned that the church had also hired a lady named Susan Maddox to assist me. I did not know her, but it would not take long to find out who she was.

With a "deer in headlights" look, I reported for duty trying to prepare myself for a mass invasion of children ages 4-12. Trying to look official and in control, I nevertheless could not mask a face that communicated, "Please don't ask me a question, I have no idea what I'm supposed to do." Fortunately, the first person I saw was Susan Oszustowicz Maddox, my assistant.

Susan was born of pure Polish ancestry having

grown up in Brooklyn, New York. She married Jimmy Maddox, an ex-Marine from Kentucky, and when I first met her, they had three children ages 6, 8 and 12. When they were married, she told Jimmy she would move anywhere in the world but Texas or Florida. Of course, the Lord brought them to Houston, Texas.

Susan was a 5'7", 115-pound package of constant motion and energy. She was totally in charge of whatever she did with a sixth sense for knowing instantly what needed to be done and then doing it. My initial thought was that although I was officially the boss, I would unofficially be working for this woman in about 6 months. I was wrong... it only took about 3 months, but the chemistry of our styles worked perfectly. The qualities I needed in a subordinate, Susan possessed, and I was able to secure the resources she needed to do her job. We partnered the responsibilities and the ministry needs were met. There was no doubt in my mind the Lord put this team together.

Susan had the behavior profile of the New Testament character, Martha ⟦S/D⟧ but the heart of her sister Mary. During the Sunday teaching time she was everywhere. She called it "whooshing" and my nickname for her became "the whoosher." But what I noticed most about Susan was her heart for children. It consumed her work. She was passionately and tenaciously committed to insuring that each Sunday School teacher had what he or she needed to teach each and every class. Totally selfless, no task was too small or too large for her to complete for a teacher. She would review each week's lesson noting the specific prop or teaching aid that was suggested. She would then see to it that it was cut out, assembled or prepared and placed in the teachers' boxes ready to be used. One lesson involved dirt. As one might guess...that next Sunday every teacher's box had a sealed plastic bag filled with dirt.

Special refreshments for the teachers were commonplace. No teacher's birthday would go by without a special celebration involving the class. She would always prepare something to eat along with birthday cards signed by all.

Although her constant activity was her trademark, she had one additional characteristic that was most unusual. Whenever a young child would have a need, she would always stop whatever she was doing and give time to that child. But it went further than that. Susan would always stoop down to the eye level of the child and patiently listen to the need and then meet it. I constantly marveled at the transition. It was truly remarkable and most effective.

After about a year, I felt it was time to suggest to the board that they hire Susan full time but she surprised me again. She had another parttime job at a Christian School that paid her in partial scholarships so that her three children could attend the school. At the school, she was known as the "lunch lady" and her role was to design the menus, secure the food services, order the lunches and collect the money. She also made sure that an extra lunch was always available for those who would otherwise go hungry.

"The lunch lady"

Typical of her style, she organized the financial figures in a logical order, concluding that the full time position would barely offset the cost of the partial scholarships. Furthermore, she was uncomfortable about giving up the bonus contact with her children. Later, I ran a check of her numbers. With what it cost her to send her children to the Christian school and what she was making, she netted less than $5 a month for herself. We kept her on parttime [really full time hours] but with a raise in pay. True to her character, she felt guilty with the extra resources.

Because my company demanded more of my time, I resigned my position as CE director knowing Susan could handle the job without me. She continued to serve in this capacity until January 1, 2000. On that fateful day, the Maddox family was traveling to visit some friends for a New Year's celebration. A neighbor boy went with them, which meant one person had to ride in the cargo area of their Ford Explorer. Susan insisted that all the children be buckled up, leaving her to ride in the rear.

At an intersection, another vehicle ran a red light and struck the Explorer broadside. Susan was thrown from her car and instantly transported to heaven at about 10:00 a.m. that New Year's day. No one else in the car was seriously hurt.

The news of the accident traveled quickly. I was informed that a special elders meeting would be held at the church to sort out what needed to be done to help the family. When I arrived, the church was packed with people. Never in my 25 years at the church had I seen this kind of response. The community, not just the church, was genuinely grief stricken, wanting to know what had happened and how to help.

A memorial service was held on the following Wednesday afternoon and the church could not hold the people. It was the largest gathering of individuals the church ever had. The outpouring of grief, respect and support overwhelmed the family. The church and community had truly lost a genuine servant leader. The next Sunday it took four people to do her job, even though all the supplies for the teachers had already been assembled by Susan.

The "why" question is a natural human response and I tried my hand at it. In order to emotionally get through it, I had to reason that the Lord must have had a more important, immediate role in heaven for Susan. In the meantime, the family is coping as best they can. A scholarship fund was set up for the children so they will be able to complete their education without a concern for financial resources. The loss of Susan is another matter. As a church, we tried our best to prayerfully offer whatever support we could and the process continues. Finally, if anyone seeks an example of a modern-day servant-leader, I can think of none finer than Susan Maddox.

While He was with us, Jesus had no place that He called home. However, He had an open invitation to stay as long as He wanted with a prominent family in the village of Bethany, about two miles from Jerusalem. This friend, Lazarus, was an influential and respected member of the Jewish community. He lived with his two sisters, Mary and Martha, who delighted in Jesus' visits to their home. Mary, the gentle one, loved to sit at Jesus' feet and listen to the Lord's teaching; whereas, Martha, the aggressive one, remained busy preparing meals.

In John 11: 1-37, the Apostle John records the events that set in motion the activities which finalized Christ's mission on earth. Starting with the death of Lazarus, verses 1-11 outline Jesus' plan to raise His friend from the dead. The simple narrative shows clearly that Jesus had a plan even before the event unfolded.

- He loved Lazarus.
- He said, "This sickness is not unto death, but for the glory of God."
- When He heard Lazarus was sick, He delayed going for two days.
- He said to the disciples, "Our friend has fallen asleep," and then had to clarify his meaning by saying, "Lazarus is dead."
- Jesus told the disciples, " I go to awaken him out of sleep."

In verse 20, Jesus finally arrives on the scene.

Martha therefore, when she heard that Jesus was coming, went to meet Him; but Mary still sat in the house.

Martha therefore said to Jesus, 'Lord if You had been here my brother would not have died!'

Martha, the active one, went out to meet the Lord, and Mary, the passive one, stayed in the house. The intensity of Martha's words, coupled with her actions, indicate an aggressive move. She couldn't wait to tell Jesus what she thought. Furthermore, by going out to meet Him, she violated the conventions and protocol of the culture at that time.

In verse 21, Martha uses a second-class conditional sentence which emphasized her perception that His absence resulted in her brother's death. Martha's directness carries a strong tone of accusation toward Jesus for not being there sooner. Although her words communicate a longing for Him to have come sooner, her tone definitely carries a reproachful message.

In verse 22, Martha tempers her disappointment with an appeal for corrective measures. Her reminder to the Lord of His resource in the Father is a combination of faith in Jesus and a last ditch effort to bring her brother back. She hasn't given up, yet it is clear later in the conversation that she really didn't expect a miracle. Certainly, Martha's emotions were running wild and her perception was that this whole event could have been prevented with a quicker response.

Representative Profile of
Martha* the sister of Lazarus

DISC PROFILE

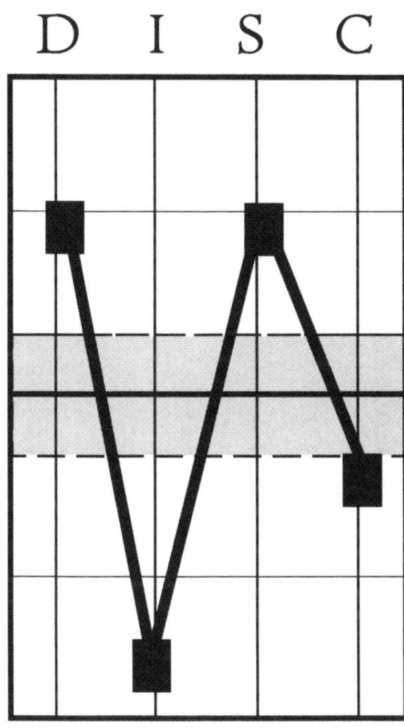

Primary Drive: Diligence in taking ownership of tasks; industrious

Personal Giftedness: Follow-through in completing a task

Instinctive Fears: Non-compliance to standards

Blind Spots: Awareness that relationships are as important as completing tasks[1]

* Based on the historical evidence, the above profiles best parallel the behavior style of Martha but is not intended to be absolute or final.

Notes:

1. Ken Voges & Ron Braund, Understanding How Others Misunderstand You workbook, ©Copyright 1999, page 78.

According to verse 23, Jesus issued a simple statement of fact that Lazarus would rise again. Martha interpreted the Lord's words as a reference to the last resurrection. She either did not have enough faith to hope Jesus would really raise her brother at this time, or His words simply struck her as only a theological statement.

In verses 25-27, Jesus responded to Martha's concerns. Jesus reminded Martha that life and resurrection is wrapped up in Him. Eternal life is bound up in faith in Him. Jesus' words spoke directly to her concerns.

I am the resurrection and the life; he who believes in Me shall live even if he dies, and everyone who lives and believes in Me shall never die. Do you believe this?

Martha replied that she believed and that she also believed He was the Messiah, the Son of God. She then went away and pulled her sister, Mary, aside and told her that Jesus had arrived and was looking for her.

In summary, the whole dialog with Martha is on an intellectual, factual, theological basis. Martha's tone was aggressive and accusatory and Jesus answered with a matter-of-fact, theological tone. It does not appear that Jesus was offended by her approach. Rather, He simply answered her concerns with a question challenging her belief in His ability to raise her brother from the dead. She appeared to be comforted by His approach.

When Mary heard that Jesus was looking for her, she quickly got up and went toward Him. However,

Representative Profile of
Mary* the sister of Lazarus

DISC PROFILE

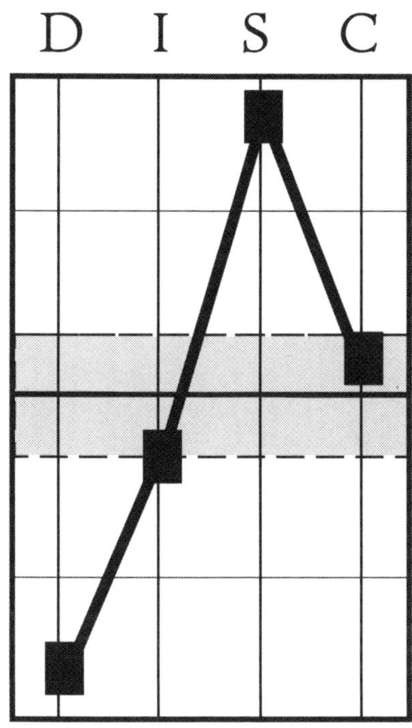

Primary Drive: Controlled, secure environment; harmony and security of the family

Personal Giftedness: Honoring those in authority; maintaining traditions

Instinctive Fears: Being strong; confronting others

Blind Spots: Being confident in knowing their pattern has strengths[1]

* Based on the historical evidence, the above profiles best parallel the behavior styles of Mary but are not intended to be absolute or final.

Notes:

1. Ken Voges & Ron Braund, Understanding How Others Misunderstand You workbook, ©Copyright 1999, page 54.

Jesus stayed where Martha had first met Him. Thinking Mary would be going to the tomb, those in the community who were consoling the family went out with Mary to see where she was going. That was not the case; she went to speak to the Lord. Observe her words!

When Mary came where Jesus was, she saw Him, and fell at His feet, saying to Him, 'Lord, if You had been here, my brother would not have died.'

When Jesus therefore saw her weeping, and the Jews who came with her, also weeping, He was deeply moved in spirit, and was troubled, and said, 'Where have you laid him?'...[and] Jesus wept.

Even though Mary used the very same conditional sentence as Martha when she met the Lord, the tone of her words likely was completely different than that of her sister. In waiting until she was summoned, she followed the proper etiquette. When she approached Jesus, she fell at His feet. Now, when she said the same words as Martha, all the while weeping, it projected grief rather than a disappointed accusation.

Even though both sisters used the same words Jesus' response was very different...each one behaviorally predictable. To Martha's High D approach, Jesus responded with facts and theology... to Mary's, High S/ Low D approach, with empathy.

"For all have sinned and fall short of the glory of God, being justified as a gift by His grace through the redemption which is in Christ Jesus."

Paul - Romans 3:23-24

Grace defined - "Unmerited favor"

The Adulteress Woman Case Study

Scripture Study
John 8:1-11

As previously mentioned, the critical measure of an effective leader is the ability to change styles as the needs and situations demand. Nowhere in Scripture is this more effectively captured than the story of the woman caught in the act of adultery. Jesus changes His style at least four times in order to resolve the spontaneous, life threatening issues placed before Him. It is a classic example of meeting individual and corporate needs which are markedly different and are being confronted in the same arena.

In John 8:2, Jesus came into the Temple and a crowd gathered to listen to Him. As was His custom, He sat down to teach them. His body language created a relaxed, yet authoritative atmosphere. In today's circles, the act of sitting down rather than standing up or over the audience creates a more conducive environment for learning. The behavioral style best able to create this environment is an I/S profile. Furthermore, the tone and words of this particular profile communicates encouragement and warmth. Jesus commonly used this style when He talked, taught and told stories to the masses. This was the setting of John 8:2. However, the environment quickly changed.

And the scribes and the Pharisees brought a woman caught in adultery, and having set her in the midst, they said to Him, 'Teacher, this woman has been caught in adultery, in the very act.

Now the law of Moses commanded us to stone such a woman; what then do you say?'

The actions of the religious leaders totally changed the environment to one of demanding confrontation. By throwing the woman at Jesus' feet, the religious leaders successfully focused all attention on the woman. Their intent was to entrap Him in a no-win situation so that they had grounds to accuse Him. Their tone was intense and orchestrated. They kept pressing for an answer because they thought they had Him. If He sided against stoning, He could be found guilty of negating the Laws of Moses. If Jesus agreed to stoning, He would be guilty of murder under Roman Law.

All too common as even today, the religious leaders manipulated the Scriptures to fit their intended outcome. They forgot to include some key details:

(1) The law was just as clear regarding the guilt of the man involved...Leviticus 20:10
(2) In the case of adultery, (involvement by a married woman), the method of death is not

specified in the Law. (Stoning was for the guilty party when a betrothed virgin and possibly the daughter of a priest, was involved.)

(3) When they quoted the Law as "such a woman" should be stoned, they intentionally used a feminine form of the word, to bolster their case against this woman. Again, the Law makes it clear that both parties were to be put to death, yet prosecution of the man was conspicuously absent.

The religious leaders were being rude, pushy and manipulative in their so-called attempt at justice. Furthermore, the Jewish system of the day had a court for such items as these and, in addition, Jesus was not the one to make such a ruling.

Sadly, the Pharisees could not have cared less about the woman. She was nothing more than a disposable object to be cast aside when Jesus fell into their trap. If she died in the process, it was of no concern to them. Jesus had a different preceptive...He saw her as a human being with value, worthy of grace being extended for her sins. However, whatever the perception, the real question is what to do next in this intense situation.

And they were saying this, testing Him, in order that they might have grounds for accusing Him. But Jesus stooped down, and with His finger wrote on the ground.

Much has been written about the Lord's response. He bent over and drew in the dust on the Temple floor. The word used can refer to either drawing or the writing of letters. So we don't know what He put on the floor. Hundreds of suggestions have been given regarding the content of His drawing. But we do know that it successfully irritated the woman's accusers, so they kept pressing for an answer.

Another way to gain insight into the text is to try and understand Jesus' actions behaviorally. From this point of view, one can possibly understand His strategy. First and foremost, the environment was emotionally charged. Clear thinking would be difficult. Furthermore, He understood they were after Him. The woman and her alleged sin really meant nothing to them. His strategy was simple...remain in control, calm down the emotion and get the focus away from the woman and onto Him. Then and only then, could He answer the accusers' question.

Jesus' actions were brilliant. Everyone expected an answer, but He deliberately ignored them, doodling in sand and projecting indifference. The result was that all eyes did, indeed, focus on Him. In this instance, Jesus' behavior best reflects the traits of a High S...calm, cool and methodical under fire.

However, aggressive individuals who demand quick action seldom appreciate these traits. They become even more intense with all their energy focused on demanding an immediate response. That is precisely what happened in this situation. If it were Jesus' strategy to get the attention focused on Himself, He obviously succeeded. However, once this was accomplished, a different behavior was now necessary to deal with the Pharisees' question.

But when they persisted in asking Him, He straightened up, and said to them, 'He who is without sin among you let him be the first to throw a stone at her.'

Again, to understand the significance of Jesus' conduct, one must look at His actions behaviorally. By standing up, Jesus created a power position ready to challenge and do battle...common behavior of High D's. His action plan fired a volley of instruction that was directed right at their collective conscience...

(1) He didn't minimize the Law

(2) He didn't negate the punishment

...but He did add a condition--the first stone had to come from one who was sinless. No one qualified. He then again changed His style.

And again He stooped down, and wrote on the ground. And when they heard it, they began to go out one by one, beginning with the older ones,...and He was left alone...

His closing arguments were very different. Jesus stooped down and wrote on the ground without saying another word. The combination of written text, coupled with silent reflection, has a chilling effect on the mind. This behavior is common among High C's and devastatingly effective when followed by dominant confrontation. With no additional words being spoken, the accusers could only reflect on His previous comments and on what He had written.

If they wanted to take the matter further, they had the option of going before the proper court; however, they would then be obligated to produce the man. Furthermore, if there was any falsehood in their testimony, the Law of Moses stated that the penalty for such statements was equal to the accusers' initial intentions...death by stoning. After processing their options in deadly silence, all the accusers suddenly reasoned that they had more important matters to attend to and retreated.

Again, the environment changed. The accusers were now gone and the woman remained where she had been all along...center stage. One can only imagine what was going through her mind at this moment...several minutes before she thought she would die and now it appeared she would be safe.

With the crowd looking on, the Lord turns His attention back to the woman. The tone of His message again changed. His address to her was not harsh but one of endearment and respect.[1]

And straightening up, Jesus said to her, 'Woman where are they? Did no one condemn you?'

The Adulteress Woman

And she said, 'No one, Lord.' and Jesus said, 'Neither do I condemn you; go your way; from now on sin no more.'

He acknowledged her using the same endearing word, "woman", that He used to address His mother while on the cross. He does not excuse her, nor is there any word of forgiveness. He calls the woman to change her life with respect to sin. Leon Morris states, "The guilty woman gave no sign of repentance or of faith. What He does is show mercy and a call to righteousness."[2] Jesus was the only sinless individual present who had the right to extend judgment on the woman for her actions. Instead, He extended His grace.

Conclusion

In this story, we see Jesus' ability to transition through all four basic behavioral styles to satisfy the needs of the situation. What is truly eye opening is "when" and "how" He does it. In teaching the people, He is an encouraging Influencer. Initially with the Pharisees' intimidating charge, He remains Steady and calm. In confronting the accusers, He switches to Dominant confrontation and finishes the mock trial with Conscientious detail.

Notes:

1. W.E. Vine, An Expeditionary Dictionary of New Testament Words, Flemming H. Revell Company, Old Tappan, NJ ©Copyright 1966, page 22.

2. Leon Morris, The Gospel According to John, William B. Eerdmans Publishing Co. Grand Rapids, MI ©Copyright 1971, page 891.

Epilogue

The Leadership Uniqueness of Jesus

Then he poured water into a basin and began to wash the disciples' feet, and to wipe them with the towel with which He was girded.

John 13:5

The Leadership Uniqueness of Jesus

Scriptural Case Study
John 13: 1-17

Servant leadership involves doing whatever task is necessary so that the needs are met. It is our opinion that Jesus is the model by which we evaluate this type of leadership. One example that clearly defines servant leadership is the act of Jesus washing the disciples' feet during the Last Supper.

John records this event in John 13. In verses 4-5, Jesus begins the process of washing the disciples' feet. It was customary at any social gathering for the host of the meal or the gathering to provide a servant to wash the guests' feet as they arrived. At this particular Passover gathering, the Lord was, in essence, the host of the meal with the disciples making the arrangements. This was a borrowed room with no official host in charge of the celebration.

The disciples should have either designated one of their group to do the washing or made provisions for someone to do it. The fact of the matter is that this practical social custom had not been a part of their plan. So, whether by oversight of the disciples, or pre-planning by the Lord, the opportunity was there for the Lord to use the situation for an illustration of a true servant attitude.

John 13:12-14, Jesus clarifies his statement.

When he had finished washing their feet, he put on his clothes and returned to his place. 'Do you understand what I have done for you?' he asked them. "You call me 'Teacher' and 'Lord' and rightly so, for that is what I am. Now that I, your Lord and Teacher, have washed your feet, you also should wash one another's feet.

When the Lord said, "Do you understand what I have done for you?", it is obvious that he meant more than the mere act of washing their feet. They knew the immediate need, because of the oversight, and that He should not have been the one to do it. Peter objected to the procedure, because he realized that the "master of the feast" never did this. Jesus is asking them if they understood the principle of serving other people's needs, even if they were not socially equal. This gesture was not symbolic, it was practical. However, it was an illustration of what they should be doing in all areas of life...serving the needs of others.

In John 13:15, 17, Jesus offers additional insight to his actions and its application to the disciples.

For I gave you an example that you also should do as I did to you...

If you know these things, you are blessed if you do them.

Jesus clarifies this principle when he states, "I have set you an example that you should do as I have done for you." Foot washing was not the issue, it was merely the example. Jesus never intended to insist on "foot washing ceremonies" as rituals within the body. He intended for his disciples to be willing to literally wash each other's feet as long as the need was there, but more importantly, to be willing to serve each other, no matter what the need might be. For the most part in this generation, we do not need our feet washed. However, we have many other needs that the Lord intends for us to meet in the lives of fellow believers. It is not "what" I have done but "as" I have done. The Lord's point is that we are to be servants of one another in the body of Christ.

Conclusion

The stories of well-known generals and political leaders were intended to illustrate the uniqueness of DISC leadership styles. It is our hope that the reader has a better understanding of and an appreciation for each of the styles. Also, having made significant, positive contributions to world history, these individuals are looked upon as heroes. Their records are their rewards in this world. Very few of us will ever get the recognition they did. However, this book was not written to elevate them but to simply show the differences in their leadership styles.

The true model of servant leadership is of course, our Lord Jesus Christ. But on the human level, we believe Susan Maddox was a wonderful example of following His pattern of serving others. It is the model of Jesus and the example of Susan that we desire to elevate and suggest to the reader to emulate. We are sure the Lord would agree.

Above all, keep fervent in your love for one another, because love covers a multitude of sins.

As each one has received a special gift, employ it in serving one another, as good stewards of the manifold grace of God.

I Peter 4: 8,10

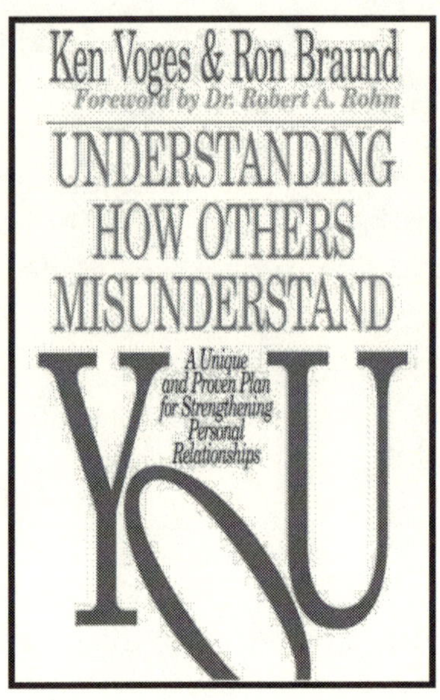

ISBN # 0-8024-1106-1

The Understanding How Others Misunderstand You book successfully incorporates the DISC model of behavioral styles with biblical principles. Fascinating case studies from Scripture give deeper insight into key Biblical characters and how God built a unique relationship with them. The textbook includes the detailed behavioral styles of 16 DISC blends and more than 32 Biblical models. This 300-page book is divided into 13 chapters and is ideal for a Bible study or personal review. Published by Moody Press, it is available through your local bookstore or In His Grace, Inc.

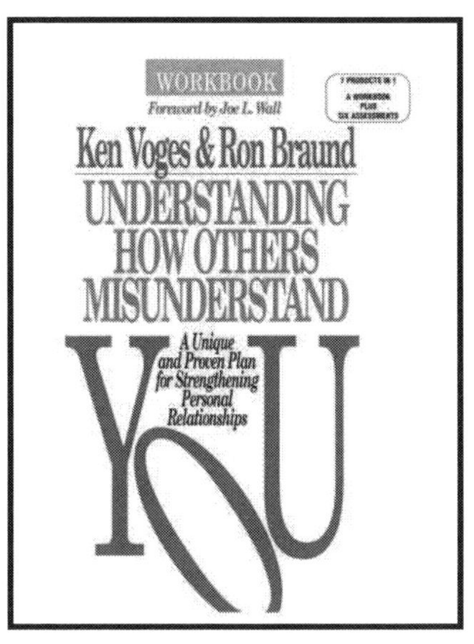

ISBN # 0-8024-1129-0

The Understanding How Others Misunderstand You workbook is the complimentary publication that visually illustrates the DISC model of behavioral styles using biblical characters. The workbook includes six instruments: four DISC surveys, Roles Analysis and Spiritual Gifts Assessment. Sixteen profiles are graphically associated with more than 32 Biblical models. This 144-page workbook is divided into 13 chapters with seven additional appendix exercises. It is ideal for retreats or Bible studies. It is distributed through Moody Press to your local bookstore or In His Grace, Inc.

About the Ministry of In His Grace, Inc.

In His Grace, Inc. was founded in 1984 by Ken Voges and exists to serve the Lord by providing believers and the Church with behavioral tools and training which assist in fulfilling the Lord's commandment to "Love one another."

Ken Voges is the original author of the Biblical Personal Profile which associates individuals in the Bible with the DISC model of behavior. This product, first published in 1985 by Performax Systems International, remains in print through Inscape Publishing. Information found in the Biblical Personal Profile remains the cornerstone resource for other products in integrating the DISC model of behavior to biblical characters. Subsequent works by Ken Voges include the Understanding How Others Misunderstand You book published by Moody Press and a workbook by the same name published by In His Grace. Both are featured on the preceding two pages.

For a complete listing and description of products and services, visit In His Grace's website which is:

www.inhisgraceinc.com
In His Grace, Inc.
3006 Quincannon Lane
Houston, Texas 77043-1201
Office - (713) 934-8810, Fax - (713) 462-2208
E-mail - krvoges@aol.com

Made in the USA
Middletown, DE
27 February 2020